*Something I want in my Life...*

*The moment I wake up*
*I want to break the chain*
*The moment I mess up*
*I want to break the chain*

*The things holding me back*
*Won't let me break the chain*
*These feelings holding me back*
*Won't let me break the chain*

*The day I cry*
*Is when I break the chain*
*The day I try*
*Is when I break the chain*

*The day I live my own life*
*Is when I'm free from the chain*

*Unknown*

# Perseverance
# Is
# Remembrance

## Authored by
## Aigner Martin

# *Perseverance Is Remembrance*

"Perseverance is Remembrance" outlines the struggles, and strength; the endurance of heartbreak time and time again. This is a true and very personal story of my life. While it may seem long, it briefly skims the troubling experiences I have had in the past with single parenthood and dating to find someone to complete me. Today, I am proud of my memories; this project has allowed me to reflect on my life and forced me to realize that people are seasonal and for good reasons. Even though Hakeem betrayed me, I share something with him that is more sacred than my own life. While Nate loved me, his love for something and someone else was much greater. And the pain I experienced as my face hit the ground will always make me remember Tony. The tales told in this book didn't capture all but it did capture enough experiences in my life to make me realize that my life is what I make it and not what anyone else says it should be. These characters are real even though the names are fictitious. My story is my legacy and the legacy of so many other single parents' today in one form or another and by sharing my personal story, I am encouraged to show others that "Perseverance is Remembrance".

> The sale of this book without its cover is unauthorized. If you purchase this book without a cover, you should be aware that it will be reported to the publisher as "unsold and destroyed." Neither the author nor the publisher has received payment for the sale of this "stripped book."

Perseverance is Remembrance. Copyright © 2011 by Aigner Martin. All rights reserved. Printed in the United States of America. No part of this book may be used or reproduced in any manner whatsoever without written permission except in case of brief quotations bodied in critical articles and reviews.

**First Edition**

*Designed* **by Aigner Martin**

**ISBN 9781461108825**

*This book is dedicated to anyone who has experienced any hardship, any heartbreak, and any lie. My hope is to encourage you to live, laugh, and love.*

**Contents**

# *Explanation Of Contents*

## *Introduction-15*

*~I Remember Me~*
*A compressed glimpse of myself and my thoughts, which you will later experience throughout this book. I pay tribute to a few remarkable projects and people for being the leading inspiration for this accomplishment.*

## *1 The Beginning Of The End-23*

*This chapter allows you to see how within a blink of an eye dreams change and people change. Life may offer you certain opportunities and depending on how you plant your seed you may be in for a surprise when you see what has grown.*

## *2 Mommy Dearest-42*

*This chapter exhibits sacrifice and love. Not all sacrifice and love comes from and ends up in a good place.*

**Contents**

# *Explanation Of Contents Continued*

## *3 The Missing Links-54*

*You will begin to see the concrete foundation that has been laid for me at this point of the book.*

## *4 "Left, Left, Left Right Left"-62*

*In order to get something you've never had, you have to do something you've never done. Something was missing from my life but by the end of this chapter I had it.*

## *5 A Dream Come True-75*

*Dreams are real and they do come into existence, It's extremely important that you watch what and how you ask for them.*

**Contents**

## *Explanation Of Contents Continued*

### <u>6 Baseball Season-93</u>

*People lie.*

### <u>7 Falling Was Easy; It Was Getting Back Up That Was Hard-103</u>

*People hurt you.*

### <u>8 His Secrets; My Lies-118</u>

*I lied. I hurt myself.*

### <u>9 Four Walls-140</u>

*Q: Why do men cheat?*
*A: Women allow them to*

**Contents**

# *Explanation Of Contents Continued*

## <u>10 Support Me, Support Me Not-153</u>

*For every action, there is responsibility.*

## <u>~The End For You; The Beginning For Me~-164</u>

*The epitome of me.*

**Perseverance is Remembrance**

# ~I Remember Me~

Reality TV shows are entertaining, don't you think? They give us a look at the unfolding drama, happening daily, in one's life. Although there are hundreds, too many to name, only a select few I can somewhat relate to.

One show happens to be "Sixteen and Pregnant." Although I was a little older than the girls on this show when I got pregnant, I'm sure the pain and embarrassment measured the same. All of the hard work I had done up until that point and the dreams I had in becoming this great doctor, were tarnished. That goes without mentioning that the love I had for my boyfriend (baby's daddy) slowly withered away. For those interested, we've all witnessed the trials that Corey and Leah faced, along with Chelsea and Adam; just to name a few.

**Perseverance is Remembrance**

Seldom do we experience, one on one, the fight and perseverance through the hardships of what seems could be the absolute worst, which Catelynn and Tyler have shown us. Like you, I've witnessed the ridicule this show has gotten from the media as well as social networks like "Facebook and Twitter." There's absolutely nothing neither funny nor horrible about this show, at all. It explicitly captures a real life aspect of the triumphs our youth faces everyday. I don't think it was meant to promote careless, sexual behavior, but rather a defense mechanism against what we may call an epidemic today, "teen pregnancy"; which in turn can and will lead to *single parenting*.

As we all know the basis of being prejudice; we also know it's not necessarily a bad thing. This very characteristic that we all possess will sometimes keep us from doing and saying certain things that may put us in compromising situations that we may later regret. I personally, will admit to this. Years ago I would take one look at girls

**Perseverance is Remembrance**

and question, how in the world they could end up pregnant, as early as middle school and high school. How does something like that happen? I snickered on behalf of their misery and held my head down in shame as they walk across the stage to receive their diplomas while supporting their huge bellies. I didn't realize what they were up against until I was facing the same reality. This show would have been an asset to my life long ago.

Another absolute favorite of mine is "Basketball Wives." Regardless of what you think about the show, I am sure you tune in every now and then. Aside from the obvious bickering and belittling of one another, they all share one thing in common. They've all struggled with maintaining an image for themselves, battled with the fate of their relationships and with endless effort, managed a nurturing home for their children. This show portrays wealthy women; married, dating or formers' of rich and handsome professionals, who are gainfully, employed in drama every other

**Perseverance is Remembrance**

day. We see gorgeous women who have no problem buying anything they want in life, but are living in moments of distress. I heard the saying "More money more problems," and this show proves that to be correct.

Perseverance is the continued effort to do or achieve something despite difficulty, failure or opposition. Another character that comes to mind in relation to the above statement is "Mrs. Melanie Barnett-Davis" played gracefully by Tia Mowry, in the hit T.V. show, "The Game." Melanie was known for her constant heartbreaking relationship with boyfriend "Derwin Davis" played by the handsome, Pooch Hall. The show portrayed Melanie as the girl who was deeply in love with her man and sacrificed basically everything she knew; her family, medical school and her individuality, in order to help him along the way in achieving his goals. How many of us have played this part in real life? And although he became successful as a football star, and married her in the *end*, it was more of the journey

**Perseverance is Remembrance**

that baffled me. The unnecessary bull shit they put each other through was more heartrending than anything; sleeping around, loving each other one minute and hating each other the next, oh and don't forget about the "baby mama" drama. The part of the dedicated girlfriend that gets shitted on time and time again is a part that we have all played. Is it worth it for the big house and nice car in the end? It may be entertaining to watch on T.V., but I guarantee you, it's no fun in real life.

Imagine falling in love with someone and being told that you love them for who they are about to become. Imagine finding out about your secretly gay boyfriend in the beauty salon. Imagine reading forums about how your child's father squandered his NFL money on random "hoochies" throughout the world and in turn can't help pay his child's medical bills. Imagine standing in the food stamp line, having your case worker talk to you as if you are beneath her, even though you know you are qualified to have her job and that she has an active case

**Perseverance is Remembrance**

herself. Imagine getting evicted from the place you and your child called "home." Twenty-six years of living and I will live on.

I recently read Steve Harvey's "Act Like A Lady, Think Like A Man." Steve did an excellent job in capturing the essence of what women should focus on in order to succeed in understanding exactly how men feel when it comes to relationships and women in general. I also believe that with all of the advice us "women" get to be perfect for that *ideal* guy, we need more seminars on how to exert that same energy into becoming *ideal* and perfect-like for ourselves. Steve mentioned the three sacred things that men strive for; who they are, what they do, and how much they make. I think these are very essential goals for both men and women. I can't ask someone who they are if I am unaware of who I am. And how many women do you hear say they can't date a man because he doesn't make a certain amount of money when their monthly income equals out to be less than their mortgage? It's important

**Perseverance is Remembrance**

that women mirror the "attraction" of true finesse. My womanhood will allow me to stand tall without doubt, honest and humble, beautiful and independent, and free of the distress I have from my own dealings with low, dishonest, ugly and dependent men, which are all qualities I saw in myself at one point. To get the best you have to give the best.

Last but not least, the amazing Jennifer Hudson is my favorite female vocalist. Her personal story, her out going spirit, and her music is an inspiration to me. "Look at my reflection, somewhere my affection, disappeared, isn't here, nothing left to say. Memories; they fading but I'm the one who made them, so I keep the love close enough to say, what if this life is all that we are given, we just can't stop livin', scared of what we'll see, cause in this world, anything can hurt you...I remember me." These lyrics are from one of Jennifer's latest cd's. That goes to say, I remember innocent life being sucked out of my body as a result of irresponsible decisions. I remember being

**Perseverance is Remembrance**

punched in my face, falling to the ground, as I witnessed my own blood drain in a sewer near by. I saw my life flash before my eyes when I sat in that clinic waiting for my HIV results. Jennifer was right, these are my memories and I'm the one who made them.

The purpose of this book served as a release. Over the course of time we all get hurt, and we all hurt others. Although we may have lingering emotions, the important thing is that we are able to forgive and let go! My anger from the past wouldn't have allowed me to accomplish this project. The body of this book entails trials that I have personally experienced and some that aren't too far from your own lives. "I remember..."

**Perseverance of Remembrance**

# 1
## ~The Beginning of the End~

It was one of the hottest months of the summer; the summer following my high school graduation, and we were about to hit the park. Hakeem was a year older than me. We attended the same high school, but didn't get along as well as we did once I graduated. We were both excited about my first year of college, especially since it was his school I had chosen to attend and therefore he could show me around. As I ran through the house trying to gather my things for our day in the sun, my mom screamed out "Hakeem, pick up the phone!" His mother, Ms. Loretta, called to tell Hakeem to come home, quick, to get some "crazy" girl out of her house. I laughed as hard as I could. Hakeem dated all kinds of girls and for some strange reason, the one's I knew of, all fell head over heels for him.

**Perseverance is Remembrance**

This particular girl was "crazy" not only because he was telling her he loved her but also because she was his first; Hakeem gave her his nut basket. He rushed home to tend to another one of his situations. I don't even remember if he ever came back that day. Although I called Hakeem my "play brother," I secretly had a crush on him and it showed in more ways than one. My mom was convinced that he liked me too but asked that we refrain from being anything other than friends.

The first semester of college rolled around and it was time for me to head down to school. My mom and I arrived at The University of Arkansas at Pine Bluff and it was everything I knew it would be. Sororities and Fraternities stomped the yard just like in the movies, and the smell of BBQ roamed the air as if I were back home. The southern hospitality made it feel just right. As for my mother, she wasn't so happy. My mom figured I could have made a better choice. She much rather I chose a school in the city versus the country so that I could

**Perseverance is Remembrance**

be accessible to the grocery stores and shopping malls; she was certain that I would not survive on the dusty roads of down south. I, on the other hand, was ready to kick it. It had been nothing but seventeen years of rules and regulations and now I was on my own.

Getting moved in was easier than I thought. Some of the Omega guys helped move me in; while they were lifting, I was admiring the view and boy was it nice. Finally after getting settled, I sent sweet kisses to my mom before I headed out to a long day of freshmen meetings. She stayed in my room to arrange things the way she thought I would like. Freshmen orientation and class scheduling lasted nearly all day. I met a few other guys and girls that were from my city and that made the time fly by even faster. After I had gotten everything straightened out with class, I was eager to get back to my room. All of my clothes and shoes had been placed in my closet and my food was in the refrigerator. My mom had fallen asleep and so waking her up wasn't

**Perseverance is Remembrance**

easy. Saying our goodbyes wasn't the easiest for her but we managed to do so.

    Hakeem greeted me upon arrival but I hadn't seen him all day. He was in football camp for hours, so I knew he would be tired when he got out. This was Hakeem's second year in college but is first year on the field. He had always been an amazing athlete so I was excited that I would continue to see him play. His dream was to one day play in the NFL and at his rate it would soon come true. Hakeem and I had a weird love/hate relationship, but somehow we managed to work through it. After a few trials and bumps in the road, we became a couple, or at least that's what it seemed like. Whatever we were, we were known around campus and that was good enough for me. Even though I was the awkward, skinny, new girl, I stood my ground when it came to anyone trying to get with my man. I didn't care about any of the previous relationships girls' had with Hakeem; I was there now and I demanded respect. Hakeem did just the same. Since I was the "football" player's

**Perseverance is Remembrance**

girlfriend, everyone found my room to be the meeting spot for everything. My new friends and I gossiped we did homework, listened to music, some even showed up looking for food; I even began to sell the care packages my mom sent for me, to make a little extra money. After a while, Hakeem put a stop to all of that. He didn't like that our male friends would randomly stop by and hang out in my room nor did he like the fact that I spent so much time with my girlfriends. He would never admit it but his color was green when it came to me and I loved it. It reassured me that we cared for each other just the same. We became very close during the time we spent together and it was honestly the best days of my life thus far. As time progressed, Hakeem and I were best friends. We talked about everything, laughed about everything, we even found ourselves praying about some things.

Hakeem had fallen asleep one day after practice and I hadn't heard from him. A few of my friend's and I ordered pizza and watched movies. It was just something to

**Perseverance is Remembrance**

do to pass time while Hakeem got his rest. Later that evening I called him to let him know I saved him some food from earlier and that I would bring it over. He was happy and said that he would meet me half way. Hakeem stayed in the football dorm and it was located half way across campus. I waited for him by the student union building. When he got there, we decided to sit there while he ate his food and spent the rest of the night talking and laughing about things that happened earlier that day. The thing I liked about Hakeem was that nothing was planned. Everything was spontaneous and outgoing about him.

Our first kiss that night was innocent and earth shattering. There was nothing weird about the connection we shared and I was grateful to have known him as nothing less than my dear friend first. I remembered skipping back to my room that night like a school girl, excited to see what awaited me in my dreams. From there, things moved swiftly between us. Even though neither of us were virgins, it definitely felt like it was first time. Hakeem invited me to his room to watch movies one evening. I was nervous because I figured it was already late so this would be our first official sleep over with one another. So of course I packed my bag; full of exotic sprays and a cute, red, laced bra and panty set. I wasn't planning to get freaky but I wanted to be prepared. One thing I should have brought along was a roll of toilet paper because it was against Hakeem's religion to have any. I noticed every time I visited him, he would always be out. Anyway the night progressed, and we didn't get half way through the movie before we were all over each other. It was a good night, and that night led to many other good nights. I'm not sure what happened but along the way Hakeem and I had done away with any use of protection. Sure, I had been taking the pill, but there would be times where I would forget or the package in the mail would be late.

Football season had begun and it was going well. I would attend every home game to support Hakeem. Unfortunately, I

**Perseverance is Remembrance**

wasn't able to attend every *away* game but we would always find time to talk when he had the chance. When I couldn't talk to him, I would either do homework or hang out with my friends. When Hakeem returned back to the campus after a weekend of being away for football, he showed up at my dorm room upset because he had heard that I had taken a walk with another guy. He yelled at me and when I tried to explain he left. I didn't understand at the time why that bothered him the way it did, he would have had to been crazy to think I would ever cheat on him or deliberately try to mess things up for us. I gave Hakeem the space he needed to calm down and he let me know when he was ready to talk again. One night after curfew had passed, Hakeem called to let me know he would be on his way. He didn't care that it was late; he just wanted to talk to me. Hakeem had become a favorite of the resident assistant in my building and on occasion she would turn her head whenever she saw him coming. My room had a wooded view; backed to nothing but dumpsters and old furniture other's

**Perseverance is Remembrance**

threw out for someone else's treasure. I lived on the second floor so we were desperately looking for a way for him to get up there unharmed. Luckily, someone's old mattress had become our treasure. Hakeem grabbed the mattress, propped it against the building, the tall way, to give him leverage into my window. As scared as I was for my six foot 200 pound boyfriend to fall and hurt himself, I didn't have any other ideas. Fortuitously, he flew in the window. After expressing to Hakeem how sorry I was and promising to never let that happen again, we indulged ourselves into a passionate night of make up sex. We ended the night with embarrassing laughs because my roommate had walked in on us as we were finishing up. We enjoyed each others arms wrapped around one another and slept soundlessly throughout the night.

    I began to notice my lack of enthusiasm for class and campus activities. My dorm room became my covenant for everything. It was hard for me to make it to class; I didn't even want to be bothered with my

**Perseverance is Remembrance**

friends anymore. I found myself gasping for air just walking down the hall to take a shower. I wanted now more than ever to be home, laying in my mothers lap. Good thing I was performing exceptionally in class because I was exempt from most of my final exams. Most of my professors seemed pretty understanding that I had become sick and I was grateful for that. My friends and I were beginning to think I contracted the flu virus since it was going around campus. I had never lived in a community based environment before and because mostly everything was shared, I was sure my immune system had crashed. My mom started to freak out because she had never been away from me when I was sick. She took every effort to mix up old remedies and send them down; still nothing seemed to work. Honestly, the only thing that made me feel better was when Hakeem was with me. He noticed my lack of excitement for anything and he tried everything to make me feel better as well. There were only so many classes he could miss and so many practices he could be late to and during

**Perseverance is Remembrance**

those times of him not being there, it was harder.

Thanksgiving break had finally come and my mom purchased me a train ticket to come home. I slept the whole way, drowning out all noise coming from my friends. It was within a blink of an eye that I was home. Seeing my mom's face warmed my heart and it made me forget that I was even sick. I figured I must have been home sick or something. My mom, however, screamed when she saw me. She was devastated because I had shaved my hair off. Being sick at school made it hard for me to maintain my hair, so off it went. She began to worry that I was now a lesbian. Even though I felt a little better, I didn't have the kind of energy my mom required, so a simple "No" to every question she asked, was all I had.

The next day she fixed my hair cut and it definitely looked better than what I had become use to at school. My mom earned a living as a hair stylist for as long as I could

**Perseverance is Remembrance**

remember and her skills were appreciated at that point. When she got finished, she told me to go upstairs to the restroom to see what was waiting for me. My mom and I had always had a special connection. Many things between us went unsaid however she always knew what to believe and what not. Like any mother, she would look at me and could tell if I was being dishonest about something. Her judgment had never steered me wrong. A "Clear Blue" pregnancy test was awaiting my arrival when I walked into the restroom; two of them to be exact. Those were the longest two minutes of my life. My mom figured I was 125 pounds when I left with long hair. She sees me now and I'm about 100 pounds, bald head, and my skin had turned pale. If I wasn't using drugs then I had to be pregnant. I saw the positive signs clearly, on both tests. But when my mom looked at them, she began to parade around the house thanking God that I wasn't pregnant. I guess initially, she was shocked and in denial but it didn't take her long to grasp onto reality and find everyway possible to resolve the situation.

**Perseverance is Remembrance**

Looking into my mom's eyes at that point was damaging for me. I knew she expected better of me and didn't want me to follow in her foot steps as a teen mom. She tried her best to make me not feel everything I was beginning to feel; shame and defeat. I saw my mom's struggle with two children and I knew, first hand, how hard it was but she never let me or my brother go without. She was a hard working woman and was blessed to have chosen a profession that allowed her to be there for us every step of the way. It was shameful that I had disappointed my family. I moved eight hours away from home just to get pregnant when it would have been cheaper to get pregnant at home. My mom's only condition to seeing me through this thing was coming home after the semester ended.

    Going back to school was hard. Aside from being sick, knowing why I was sick really messed with my head. My mom wanted to tell Hakeem's mother right away, but I begged her not to. I wanted to talk things over with him first and give him a

**Perseverance is Remembrance**

chance to speak with her himself. Plus, I knew I didn't want to keep the baby anyway, so I didn't see a need in getting everyone involved in a *possible* situation. Hakeem came to see me once I arrived back at school.

He was calmer than I thought, and we talked through various scenarios to try and make the situation we were in benefit the two of us. Hakeem didn't agree with me going back home, he suggested that we move off campus into our own apartment. He figured I could take online courses and he could still attend school. That was an option, but it wasn't my favorite. I didn't know anything about raising a child nor did I want to learn. I didn't see children in my future. Hakeem's biggest fear was telling his mother that I was pregnant. I told him my mom was only going to give him so long to break the news to her. It was added pressure for the both of us knowing my mom lived ten minutes away from Ms. Loretta and could break the news to her at anytime. My final decision was to terminate

**Perseverance is Remembrance**

the pregnancy; my mom would pay my half and Hakeem's mother would pay his half, if she ever found out.

    One evening as my friends and I kick back in my dorm room, my phone rang. "I think we need to talk" were the words that smacked me in my ear. These are words that no girl wants to hear especially coming from another female who claims she is in a relationship with your boyfriend. I placed her on speaker phone so that I had witnesses to prove I wasn't crazy. Do you want to know who the girl was? It was the "crazy" girl from the summer; the one Hakeem had to rush home to put out of the house. Long story short she was allegedly Hakeem's girlfriend. She claimed they had never broken up and they were very much in love with each other. My first concern was "How the hell she got my number?" I had never seen or talked to this girl in my life. Along with a relationship, comes sex, right? Well, she said they were definitely still sleeping with one another and were not using protection. In my mind, I was thinking

**Perseverance is Remembrance**

"Was this girl pregnant too?" She went on to say how hurt she was when she found out he had another girlfriend and didn't understand how that was possible. Of course she had questions for me and I told her everything she wanted to know, except that I was pregnant. She apparently tried calling Hakeem several times before she called me, but he wasn't answering her calls. I told her that I would go talk to him and have him call her shortly. In the beginning, my heart went out to her. I had never received a phone call like that before and it was sad to hear her crying and upset over something she definitely had no control over. I can remember saying to my friends after I got off the phone with her, "This helfa is upset because of a title, wait until she finds out I'm pregnant."

After mixing up an old remedy of bleach for Hakeem, half way across the campus I marched, with my friends marching right behind me. They begged me to let it go and wanted me to consider the fact that the girl could have been lying. I

**Perseverance is Remembrance**

had already considered that, but it wasn't her that bothered me. I trusted Hakeem. He was my friend first before anything else. I thought we had the kind of relationship to where we could discuss anything. It was hurtful for another woman to call me and tell me anything about my man. Whether it was true or not, it needed to be addressed. Hakeem had been warned that I was on my way and I was not happy.

He came outside when I got there, and while I wanted to automatically believe him without a word, I asked that he call her. Hakeem didn't know exactly what had been said by that point but he proceeded to call his "girlfriend." Now whether she was actually on the other end of the phone is still unknown. He told her that she was lying, and that I was his only girlfriend and urged her never to call me or him again. I was so angry that night; him saying that to her did absolutely nothing for me. I wondered what her deal was, and why me? I figured someone both Hakeem and I knew had given her all of this information about

**Perseverance is Remembrance**

us and she would soon find out that I was not just his girlfriend but I was his pregnant girlfriend, and that would surely send her over the top. I was positive that when she did find out she would roll right on over to Ms. Loretta's house to tell her the breaking news, and while she did so, someone else had beat her to it.

Eighteen years old was not an age for anyone to become a mother or father. I had planned on becoming a clinical psychologist and earning my PhD. And Hakeem was to graduate with his criminal justice degree and pursue his dream of playing for the NFL. Unfortunately, my mom forfeited her end of the bargain, agreeing to pay for my half of the abortion. She said that if Hakeem and I could come up with the money on our own, then we were free to get it done. How was I to do it? Neither of us a job and I could sell fifty care packages and still not have half of the money. Within a blink of an eye, my dreams had changed. This child was now my seed and I had to do everything possible to nurture it. This was truly the beginning of the end of who knows what kind of relationship Hakeem and I could have had and the life I should have had.

# 2
## ~Mommy Dearest~

Those nine months weren't the dream of any expecting mother. When I thought of "pregnancy," I thought of happiness, togetherness, family, and excitement. It was the opposite for me. I wasn't happy, Hakeem and I were drifting apart, and our families were feuding; making it difficult for us to get along. I hadn't had much communication with Hakeem or his mother during my pregnancy.

Ms. Loretta didn't believe that Hakeem was the father of my child and suggested that a few other guys would better fit the profile. After hearing several insults she had made toward me, I temporarily counted her out of my already stressful life. Hakeem would come home to visit me every now and then and call when he had the chance. I

**Perseverance is Remembrance**

wasn't comfortable with Hakeem seeing me because I had gained an excessive amount of weight and I didn't feel like I would be anyone he would be attracted to anymore. He did his best by telling me how pretty I still was to him, but my confidence had already begun to sink.

    I was two days away from my due date and I didn't feel like I was any closer to going into labor. My doctor fussed at me an awful lot those few weeks because I was over weight and he was worried it would do harm to the baby. He told me that if I didn't lose five pounds in the next two days, he would have no choice but to induce my labor. So what did I do? I ate more! Ms. Loretta, surprisingly, called to ask if she could take me out to lunch. I accepted. I was nervous because this was the first time we had spoken the whole time I was pregnant. My real comfort came from knowing I would be eating Red Lobster that day. I didn't know what this meeting would be like but I was interested in knowing her approach.

**Perseverance is Remembrance**

When we got there, she encouraged me to order whatever I wanted and I did just that. While I ate, she basically talked about how this whole situation came about. I understood she was hurt which is why I kept my distance that entire time. Apparrently she and Hakeem had numerous discussions about the paternity of the baby, and while I was confident he didn't doubt me, it was her who did. She had come to the conclusion that she would not ask for a paternity suit. It was nice of her to tell me that however I didn't plan on offering one had she asked anyway. Hakeem and I were both aware that we spent countless, condom-less nights together and it was nobody's, not even our parents, place to come into our situation and dictate what was going to happen. By the end of our lunch, I was fine with Ms. Loretta.

It was hot out, so just being outside drained every bit of energy I had. She was driving, so we ended up back at her house after our lunch. Hakeem was there, and I was happy to see him. We sat on the couch

**Perseverance is Remembrance**

together and watched TV. He rubbed my large stomach and as we talked to one another he dosed off. Hakeem snored like an angry bull. I had become use to this annoying sound of his however it go on my nerves that night. He was scheduled for surgery the very next day because he had been diagnosed with sleep apnea. It was suppose to sooth his snoring and allow him and others around him to rest peacefully. I got past the sound after it felt like someone had taken a knife to my lower back. Every time I tensed up, Hakeem would wake and ask me if I were ok. I nodded yes, but I was in pain. He massaged my back but nothing worked. I told him to ask his mother to take me home.

On the ride home, tears trickled from the right side of my face as I stared out of the passenger's window. As soon as Ms. Loretta pulled in front of my mom's house I rolled out of the car without even saying goodbye. I walked briskly to the door and as I did so, there went my bladder. I wasn't sure if I was over excited or what. When I

**Perseverance is Remembrance**

entered the house, I ran to my mom and asked her to rub my back. Unluckily, my mom had been sipping on some coolers earlier that evening and she was heavily intoxicated. I'm still not sure how that was possible but it happened. She urged me to drink a glass of water and lay down. I did so and that still did nothing for me. The pain was becoming more and more intense and I couldn't catch my breath.

    I stood, towering over my mom as she laid in her bed, trying to recover from what seemed like a joke to me. I screamed "Mama!" She jumped up and said "Oh my God, I think you are in labor!" She told me to keep track of my contractions and she would call my doctor. He told us to head to the hospital; I had been in labor for hours before I had realized it, but my water still hadn't broke. My cousin rushed right over to help me out, but it was really my mom who needed the help. Right when I thought we were already to go, my mom realized she ran out of the house without putting any underwear on. And as my contractions grew

**Perseverance is Remembrance**

closer and closer together, we waited for her to run inside and find some. My cousin was in charge of calling everyone on my list to get them to the hospital but Hakeem never answered. I encouraged her to keep on calling, she wasn't aware of his sleeping condition. Ms. Loretta eventually answered the phone and assured us that they would be on their way to the hospital. She said she figured there was something wrong with me earlier and wondered why I hadn't said anything. I honestly didn't think I was labor!

Upon arrival, the doctor examined me and reported that I was five centimeters dilated. I figured five down, five more to go. Once Hakeem arrived to the hospital, I could tell he looked as if he wanted to take all of the pain away. There was nothing he could do. I was eventually moved into the delivery room because within a few hours I had dilated to eight centimeters. I grew more anxious the closer it got for me to deliver. Ms. Loretta helped plenty of people before deliver their babies, so it was comforting to know she was there with me

**Perseverance is Remembrance**

and my mom. My mom was a complete wreck. She drank coffee all night and fussed at me that I listen to the doctors and push as hard as I could so "her" baby could make it safely into the world. The "hormonal" me wanted to have her removed from the room.

Hours passed by and I was still only eight centimeters. Hakeem's surgery was scheduled and he had to be there to get the procedure done; no excuses. Apparently he rescheduled several times before, posing a serious risk to his health. He and Ms. Loretta left the hospital so that he could get prepped for surgery and hopefully make it back for the birth of our child. Soon after, a nurse rushed in the room and after seeing the monitor she rushed back out. Minutes later followed several other doctors along with the tools needed to deliver a baby. I was not ready; I needed Hakeem to be there. The baby's heart rate begun to decrease, so the doctor's moved quickly to get the situation under controlled. When I noticed them unhooking me from the medicine that was stabilizing my contractions, I freaked out. My mom rushed to call Ms. Loretta because she knew she would be better at helping me than her. I felt nothing when I began to push because of the numbing epidural. I had to work twice as hard and I was exhausted.

Ms. Loretta arrived just in time and she helped me along while my mom yelled at me from afar. She paced the delivery room, holding her head and screaming the entire time. Finally, she was here. Eighteen hours and fifty-four minutes of labor and our baby girl was here. Sadly, Hakeem missed the actual birth, but his hospital was able to rush him right over afterwards. Six pounds, seven ounces of pure innocence; this is what I had been waiting for. Ms. Loretta took the honors of cutting the baby's umbilical cord in place of Hakeem. Her first words to me were "Oh my God, she looks just like Hakeem." When I saw Hakeem, I could tell he was in a lethargic state. He had been instructed not to speak because it would put strain on his throat and cause

**Perseverance is Remembrance**

him to bleed. Looking at his daughter for the first time brought tears to his eyes. He leaned over to me, kissed me on my forehead and painfully whispered "She's beautiful, thank you."

    Although I initially had the help of my mom, Hakeem and his mother, I still had no idea what I was doing. That "infant 101" crash course they gave me at the hospital did no good. I didn't even feel like I had a connection with my own child. It was like my mind; thoughts and individuality was clouded into this fog, and I didn't know which direction was the right direction. I was also sad because I knew Hakeem would be leaving me and the baby. His summer breaks weren't much of a break at all because football players had to report early for camp. Hakeem was very helpful when he was there. He took on the majority of the responsibility allowing me to rest more often during the day. When he left, my mom took on a major role for me and the baby.

**Perseverance is Remembrance**

Sadly to say, Hakeem and my relationship began to change noticeably. I'm sure the thought of a new baby in his life was stressful however it was me who was actually dealing with it first hand. I won't lie; apart of me was jealous that Hakeem was able to continue on with his life as he knew it before. Why did I have to forfeit school and stay home with this child alone? The thought of Hakeem down at school without me definitely bothered me. I couldn't handle that we lived in different states. From then on, we argued a lot. It became difficult for either of to trust one another and therefore our relationship as we knew it was rapidly deteriorating. We hear stories, see movies and read books about this very scenario. I didn't want to be hurt by Hakeem and figured I would prepare myself for the worse. I eventually forced myself to be okay with the fact that our relationship would end. Looking back I'm not so sure that was the right thing to do. Hakeem would call and visit us often and then not so often.

My mom encouraged me to get out of the house. It had been a full six weeks that

51

**Perseverance is Remembrance**

I had been inside and I was near losing my mind. Mom was old fashioned and believed that a woman's body needed time to heal from such stress. Though it was upsetting leaving the baby the first few times, it was what I needed. I decided to look for a job. I thought that working would give me the little independence I needed to allow myself to feel adequate enough to provide for my baby girl. My mom helped out a lot, but I didn't want her to take on my responsibility. I knew she would help me more when she saw me helping myself. After succeeding at finding a job, I wanted to get back in school.

The community college was nothing like what I had become use to but it gave me the poise I lacked. I didn't want to be another statistic in my community. Teen moms were multiplying and the chances of them continuing their education were slim to none. I wanted to build a strong work ethic and gain the specific skills it took to earn my college degree. State assistance was an alternative however too many

**Perseverance is Remembrance**

worked it as if it were a full time job and I did not want to fall in that category. Work and school along with a new born baby was hard but it taught me my first lesson in life; perseverance.

My mom and I had fallen into a rough patch. I decided to take my daughter and leave. Ms. Loretta let us stay there until things blew over, and that was hard. After six classes, eighteen credit hours and five A's and one B, I went back home. That argument between my mom and I was the push I needed to know that I could do anything and succeed at it. It didn't take me much longer to start thinking about my long term finances. A part time job as a cashier wouldn't provide what I had in mind for my family. I needed secure benefits for me and my family and considering the position I had been put in, I couldn't wait for anyone to step up. Approaching the end of my first year of community college, I resigned from my job and enlisted in the United States Army.

# 3
## ~The Missing Links~

I think back to when Hakeem and I were in high school. As I mentioned before, we didn't really get along. It was more like a love/hate relationship. The crazy thing is that I dated his best friend. Brandon and I got together when I was fifteen years old. Overall, he was a really cool guy, but after finding pictures of him and other girls (one being Hakeem's high school girlfriend at the time) we didn't last through school. Hakeem and Brandon were inseparable; if you saw one, you always saw the other. I knew that Brandon would complain to Hakeem about our issues; typical issues couples' our age had. To the naked eye, it did seem as if I was always fussing at Brandon about things he wasn't doing right. But that was because he wasn't doing them right! I secretly knew that Brandon wasn't being faithful to me like he professed. On several occasions, Hakeem

**Perseverance is Remembrance**

witnessed me yelling at Brandon in front of his locker and therefore thought I was the girlfriend from hell. Clandestinely, Hakeem liked me, I was sure of it. There was this one incident in the field house...but that's a story for another day. Nevertheless, we somewhat shared a mutual circle of friends and from time to time we would all get together and hang out.

My mom, not so much, but Hakeem's mother, Ms. Loretta, seemed really nice. She was easy to talk to, fun to be around and she and Hakeem seemed to have had a really good relationship with one another. In addition, Hakeem's family was heavy into church. He had invited me to some church events that his mother was in charge of and from then on, I was impressed. I had grown up in church as well, but the doctrine taught didn't capture my attention as well as Hakeem's church did. I eventually made the switch. While it was difficult to talk to my mom about my pregnancy, it was much more complicated for Hakeem to tell his mother. I tried buying him time with my

**Perseverance is Remembrance**

mom; I just didn't think he knew what to say and how to say it. I'm not so sure he even wanted to.

While the "crazy" girl had told Ms. Loretta that I was pregnant, it was my mom who had beat her to it. My mom didn't want to be an accessory to me and Hakeem's secret. She felt as if it were only fair that his mother know, and while she gave him time to tell her, his time wasn't her time. She drove over to Ms. Loretta's house, knocked on her door and revealed to her that her son was expecting a child. Like any mother, she was hurt and couldn't believe that any of it was true. According to my mom, she was in complete shock. Ms. Loretta seriously doubted that was correct and stated that Hakeem would never do anything like that. She professed that her son went to church, was saved; sanctified, and filled with the precious gift of the Holy Ghost and therefore was a virgin, so he couldn't have fathered anyone's child. My mom assured her that I too, was raised in church however she knew her child well enough to know that I was capable of making mistakes nor was I too high up on any pedestal for her, my own mother, to recognize them. My mom showed pride in her kids but she would never cover up for our wrong doings or admit that we weren't capable of such. My mom figured she had time to deal with the situation and now it was Ms. Loretta's turn to deal with it. She left that day with one thing in mind and one thing only, that her daughter would be taken care of.

Tension was definitely high between Hakeem and his mother. He wasn't allowed to come home for a while and hence had to go stay with friends when he was off from school. When things blew over with them, it didn't take long for me to hear that she implied that a few other guys were more likely the father of my baby, one of the guys being Brandon. She wanted a paternity test and I refused. I didn't believe that it was Hakeem who doubted me, but for anyone to put an ounce of doubt in his mind, hurt me. I walked around discouraged and

**Perseverance is Remembrance**

embarrassed for the duration of my pregnancy. I was sad and I cried just about everyday up until the baby was born. I hadn't received one phone call from Ms. Loretta throughout those eight months. My mom coordinated a huge baby shower, inviting my family and friends. It was unfortunate but because of the disconnection between the families, I didn't feel comfortable calling Hakeem's family to invite them. I honestly felt as if his mother didn't care or was still too hurt to deal with what was soon to be our reality. Although Ms. Loretta was a huge help in the delivery room, to both me and my mom, she had no problem with letting me know how business would be conducted regarding the caretaking of my baby.

Immediately following our baby's birth and the departure of everyone, she informed me that Hakeem would not be leaving school to work any "penny earning" job in order to provide for this baby. She went on to say that if I needed anything for the baby, don't ask Hakeem for anything,

**Perseverance is Remembrance**

she needs to be the person I come to. Oh really? I was insulted that she felt the need to tell me that. My hormones were all over the place and my feelings were left hurt. The only thing I could say was "okay." Hakeem sat there, listened but didn't say a word.

Growing up, just about every little girl wants to be the best mommy in the world. Me, on the other hand, I wanted to be the best doctor in the world. I never intended to have kids and the fact that my intentions had just been compromised, I didn't plan on doing this alone; I didn't feel I should have had to. Like I said before, my mom helped out tremendously. She made sure that we didn't go without our necessities. Even though my mom took care of us, and my part time job helped out a little, there were still things I went to Hakeem for and unfortunately, I couldn't get them because he wasn't *able* to work. I wasn't willing to comply with Ms. Loretta's wishes by no mean. The way I saw things were, if I had to ask my daughter's father for something

**Perseverance is Remembrance**

that she needed, and he didn't have it, it was up to him to find out how to get it. I was definitely grateful that Ms. Loretta anticipated on being a part of her granddaughter's life; however I felt as if she completely over stepped her boundary as *just* the grandmother, and directly implied that she will be the sole provider for my child. I can run down a long list of altercations with Ms. Loretta leading to this very day however this one marks where our misunderstanding for one another initially derived.

My decision to enlist into the military wasn't to leave my child or to run away and have the "fun" I longed for. As a matter of fact, I didn't see fun in my future. I had basically been told that I would be taking care of my child on my own, without the aid of Hakeem, so I had to make some serious changes. I honestly never wanted Hakeem to quit school; I wanted him to succeed like I had planned to do. I simply wanted him to help contribute to our creation. My mom feared what would be ahead when it came to my dealings with Hakeem and Ms. Loretta, but I assured her that Hakeem wasn't the bad guy. I knew that as time went on and our daughter grew, he would realize what it truly meant to be a father; a provider and he would tell his mom to back the hell up.

It was hard being a mother at the age of eighteen. I realized that men and women make the ultimate sacrifices for their children. It's not the genetics that title you "mom and dad." It's the time that you take to build a relationship, the tears you shed, the good times and bad times that bring families closer together. My mom said that if Hakeem continued to allow his mother to speak for him the way he had, that he would never be good a enough man or father for me and her granddaughter.

# 4
## ~Left, Left, Left Right Left~

Once I successfully completed my first year of community college, it was time for me to put my army greens on. It was absolutely devastating seeing my little girl cry as hard as she did. She wasn't sure what was about to happen, but the tight grip of a one year old clutching onto my pants assured me that she knew something was about to happen and it wasn't good. Hakeem surprised me by coming down to support my departure. That, beyond a doubt, meant something very special to me. I didn't think he was going to show up, because I knew he disagreed with my choice to enlist. Although my mom was there, like always, to help out with the baby, it made me feel even better knowing that her dad was there to console her as well.

**Perseverance of Remembrance**

It was a long ride to South Carolina. I flew on plane after plane and rode bus after bus. When I arrived, I wished the journey had been longer, for I was sure I was in hell. There were drill sergeants lined up and down the dusty road ready to attack. I couldn't understand why they were so angry, I was sure they would've been happy to see us! It was already midnight, and after about 10 hours of torture, we were finally able to rest. It had been a long process of medical screenings, running through obstacle courses and more and I was just ready to take a long nap. It took a few weeks for me to get totally into the routine they had given us, I adjusted just fine.

A typical day: 3:30am wake up, physical training, showers, breakfast, field training, more physical training, dinner and lights out. These days lasted anywhere from fourteen to eighteen hour days. I looked forward to the little personal time we were granted. I was able to read letters from my family and even though it made me sad, I

**Perseverance is Remembrance**

was happy to know that I had finally made them proud. Sorry to say, my grandfather passed away and I wasn't able to ease the stresses on my family. I knew he was ill before I left home however his death seemed sudden to me. I was sad because I knew I wasn't able to go home and share my stories with him. I worried that my performance in training would be affected but due to the support my peers lent me, I was able to make it through.

My mom also informed me of an altercation that happened with Hakeem and Ms. Loretta, concerning our daughter. Apparently the police was involved and this was stress I did not need. Overall, my mom was upset that Hakeem still hadn't stepped up his financial contribution for his daughter. Ms. Loretta felt as if finances weren't as important as Hakeem spending time with his child. With the money I was earning, I made sure it was accessible to my mom so that she was able to properly care for our baby. Hakeem and I wrote to each other as well. Talking to him served as

**Perseverance is Remembrance**

an escape from all of the training for me; I still wished that I was down there with him at school. He informed me that college life was nothing special but most of all he missed me, and I missed him too. I never told him, but there wasn't a night that passed that I didn't sleep with one of his letters.

After a long journey and building friendships with the people I grew to love, basic training was over and it was time for all of us to graduate. My family flew hundreds of miles to witness me take the victory march across the field that millions before me had done. It was truly an honor. I spent most of my nights crying because I missed my family. I wondered if I was making the right decision. Unhappily, I missed my baby's second birthday and that ripped me apart. I could remember writing her a letter on a piece of notebook paper, letting her know how much I loved her and missed her. I drew a few balloons on there to make it happy for her. As tears from my eyes drowned the letter, the ink became

**Perseverance is Remembrance**

unreadable.

    Immediately following graduation, I ran across the field to greet my family. I saw them before they recognized who I was. My mom didn't expect that I would be so skinny, losing all of my "baby weight." My skin darkened dramatically due to the suns favor on my skin in the hot Carolina's. I didn't expect for my mom to be looking like a celebrity, gliding across the grassy field with a silk umbrella and silk shoes; I was sure the money I sent home was put to good use. I said "Damn, silk mama?" She laughed. My daughter had grown beautifully and was beginning to talk. I knew I had some catching up to do. Tears began to run down my face because I was so excited to see them, I had been away for three months and that feeling of happiness was worth every bit of it. I began to cry a little harder when I saw, what looked like a chandelier in my daughter's newly decorated room while flipping through some pictures my mom had brought with her. We weren't rich, but I was starting to think my

**Perseverance is Remembrance**

mom was. I didn't complain, I was just happy to provide for them both however I advised my mom to hold it down on the spending! I needed to live too when I got back home. Knowing my daughter's position gave me the security I needed to move on to round two. Now that basic training was complete, it was time to tackle AIT, my job training.

From South Carolina, up to Virginia I went. There was no time wasted getting from one obstacle to the other. Since basic training, we had all earned certain privilege's we didn't have before, for instance, wearing civilian clothes on the weekend, whereas before we absolutely had to wear our uniforms seven days a week. We were also allowed to have cellular phones. I could talk to my family and Hakeem as much as I wanted, whereas before we only communicated through letters. AIT was like college; it was actually fun. Yes, we still had to work hard but we played even harder. I remember one weekend our drill sergeants loaded us all up

**Perseverance is Remembrance**

and took us to Busch Gardens; it was a reward for a week well done! I resided in a huge dorm, males on one side and the females on the other. Our drill sergeants weren't as cold hearted as the ones from basic training. Instead of field training most of the day, our lessons now took place inside of the classroom. It was fourteen weeks of computers and continuous tests and there was no room for mistakes.

While fraternizing was prohibited, it was much easier to do so. Soldiers weren't allowed to date soldiers and soldiers weren't allowed to date drill sergeants. You would've had to been a fly on the wall in some of the hotel rooms on the weekend. Funny thing is that I once heard that our food was cooked with a certain ingredient that suppressed our sexual appetite. I'm not sure how true that was, but if you ask me, it wasn't strong enough; we needed more! Some people, even my closest friends, were stressed because of the lack of intimacy they were able to share with their loved ones since they were so far away. I've

**Perseverance is Remembrance**

witnessed cheating girlfriends and boyfriends, and cheating wives and husbands.

One afternoon, while doing our daily chores, formation was called by the duty sergeant. We regularly kept accountability all of bodies and weapons. Strolling out of the building walked this tall, dark skinned, strong looking gentleman. I couldn't really see his eyes, because his drill sergeant hat was tipped so far toward the tip of his nose. His teeth clenched his bottom lip, leaving his gold K-9's exposed to the sun, where the light reflected, nearly blinding everyone in sight. His military bearing looked perfect; his uniform was nice and crisp, and his boots were laced to impress. His skin looked so smooth just the way I liked. Right when I decided to step outside of the formation to get a better look, the thunder from his voice suggested that "attention" was the only position I needed to be standing at. He screamed at the top of his lungs, cursing us all out; he was furious. I was immune to this kind of behavior from the drill sergeants

**Perseverance is Remembrance**

however I could tell that this one actually had a *reason* to be upset.

Someone had left their weapon unattended to earlier that day and given that he was the duty sergeant he was held responsible for all actions. Since day one, we were all reminded time and time again about the importance of our sensitive items; weapons were high up on that list. We painfully stood in formation for a few hours until the guilty party stepped forward to claim their weapon and accept their fate. We were then dismissed from formation and ordered back to our chores. It was already hot, so I tried to run as fast as I could back to my room without anyone stopping to talk to me. I was really hoping to miss the front desk; the duty sergeants desk. That was a total fail.

Soon as I passed by, the duty sergeant yelled "Wait a minute private, get your ass back here." I quickly thought about what I had done wrong, and nothing came to mind. He then said "How come I haven't seen you

**Perseverance is Remembrance**

here before, who are you?" I didn't have an answer for him; I wondered the same thing. I had been in AIT for weeks now and I didn't remember him ever being assigned to my company. Once we acquainted ourselves with one another, we learned that we were from the same city, born and raised. After a few more run-in's with him, I realized I was smitten over my drill sergeant, and I knew that was unacceptable. So what was I to do about this man?

I would try my best to dodge him at night when I was assigned to patrol, I tried not looking directly at him during formation, I would even find alternate routes around base so that we wouldn't run into each other and be forced to talk to on another. It was nerve wrecking because he hinted in more ways than one that he was interested as well. Up unto this point I had done well with staying away from any trouble; his rank simply wasn't worth the risk or my possible prolonged stay away from home. Some of my friends even began to notice how I was constantly singled out and made

**Perseverance is Remembrance**

fun of during formations, picked for the "luxury" duties everyone wanted; they became suspicious. Of course for a while I acted as if nothing was different, but the temptation got the best of me. Although I never revealed anything to my closest friend, it became obvious to more than enough that we both had broken the code. The one night that we spent together was the *only* night. But detailed in that evening, was infatuation. Just the thought of doing something that was forbidden excited me and although we grew to have feelings for one another, I was convinced that things between us would never work. I refused to jeopardize his and my job as well as live in secrecy. He reassured me that things would get better but deep down inside I knew I was going home to a bigger mess. He was aware of my situation with Hakeem and my child and he was confident that he could make me happy. He probably would've done just that had he not been married.

Time was flying and it was time for me to see my family again. The graduation

**Perseverance is Remembrance**

ceremony was much smaller this time and ended quickly. So therefore my mom and my aunt were my only visitors but I enjoyed every bit of them both. It was sad saying goodbye to all of the many friends I became to love and respect. We all exchanged numbers and email addresses and promised to keep in touch forever. The flight back home was long and agonizing. I was eager to see my little girl, especially since she wasn't able to come to my graduation. By the time I arrived back home, none of my luggage accompanied me at the airport. It appears that a big, army green duffle bag looked suspicious, and had to be kept in another city for clearance. Yea, whatever; I was just happy to be home. I was nervous to walk in my mom's house, but I bolted through the front door and there she was; standing their with her arms wide open. She immediately led me to her newly "princess" decorated room. As I enjoyed the first moments of my invitation into her world, I looked on her wall and saw, in a frame, the piece of notebook paper I mailed home for her birthday. The evidence from my tears

**Perseverance is Remembrance**

traveled far and it was there to remember for years to come. This was our new beginning; I had done this for her. What was missing? I knew, but what I gained? I didn't, but it was something innovating, something I would need.

# 5
## ~A Dream Come True~

Home was nothing like what I had become use to for the past year. I didn't have to get up early anymore, no more long runs and no more diets. Even though I didn't have my drill sergeants "motivating" me, I still found myself keeping up with my structured routine.

Since I resigned from my job before leaving home, I needed to find another one. My military job was worked once a month but I needed more income. It wasn't hard doing so; I had learned many skills over the past year while I was away and that became my advantage when job hunting. I applied to a civilian job similar to my military profession and was made an offer right away. Hakeem was next on my "to do" list. Our relationship had pretty much ended by that point. He was honest with me about dating another girl at school and while I was

**Perseverance is Remembrance**

hurt at the time, I found myself completely fine with it. I missed Hakeem and wanted to see him anyway. Due to some family quarrels, he and his mother had limited time to spend with our baby while I was away. Before leaving, I granted my mom legal guardianship over my daughter. It was primarily to ensure her safety and to enable that certain decisions could legally be made for her. I thought it was the best decision but Ms. Loretta figured it was only fair that I left that responsibility in Hakeem's hands. I didn't see how that would work being as if he wasn't *able* to work to support her. What she really meant, is that I should've left our daughter in her hands to be looked after. My mom and I agreed that she would allow Hakeem to see his child no matter what. She wanted him to be an active father in her life, she still couldn't get over the fact that Ms Loretta was as intrusive as she was on Hakeem's behalf. I didn't really know all of the details and I didn't want to. I figured it was water under the bridge so the next day, I rushed right over to Ms. Loretta's house.

**Perseverance is Remembrance**

Hakeem expected me to be there; he was on his way home from school. Although we weren't together anymore, our greeting for one another made it feel like just the opposite. His touch against me was warm and felt stronger than ever. I enjoyed spending time with him and our daughter. It actually felt like we were a family, after all, that's all I really wanted. We planned an eventful day full of activities. Of course Ms. Loretta tagged along, but afterwards Hakeem and I dropped her and the baby off at home and we enjoyed time to ourselves. We went to a movie, took a walk in the park, and spent the rest of the evening laughing and telling jokes about one another. It felt good to be in his presence once again. He expressed that while he was upset about my leaving, he was proud of what I had accomplished. That meant a lot to me. I too, was proud of what he was accomplishing. He was nearing the completion of his college degree and working hard to pursue his dream of playing in the NFL. He got me to understand that his sacrifice was not quitting school. He

**Perseverance is Remembrance**

made it clear that his daughter was his motivation for working hard on and off the field so that he was able to provide the life he wanted for her. I respected and loved him for that. It reassured me that despite the odds of our dealings with one another, he would still be the man and the father I had prayed for. I was in this despicable battle between who my mom *thought* he was and who he *told* me he was going to be. I wasn't sure of how serious he was with his relationship with that girl; I figured no too serious because we ended that night with passion and sweet kisses to the forehead. Hakeem, soon after, headed back down to school to prepare for what awaited him.

Being back at home seemed different for me. I realized that I left with nothing and came back with something. I didn't quite know what that something was, but it was innovating and I definitely noticed a change. It didn't take me long to adjust to my new job. After I started working and seeing what I was capable of doing with my

**Perseverance is Remembrance**

money, I figured it would be best for me to search for me and my daughter a place of our own to live. Living with my mom was great and it helped me out a lot, but I wanted to feel like a real working mom.

My mom was sad; she had gotten use to the soft cries and happy giggles of her grandbaby, but she was confident that I could handle such a responsibility on my own. Plus, I knew if I were to ever stumble she would be there to help me up. It took me weeks, but I found the perfect townhouse for us. Just when I thought things were going in my favor, the unimaginable happened. My performance level at worked dropped below what was considered "acceptable." I became fatigued from standing too long and nausea provoked my body at the thought of food. Does any of this sound familiar? That last night of passion with Hakeem turned into a seven week old fetus growing inside of me. How could we have been so careless, again? I didn't waste any time telling Hakeem. I couldn't believe that I was pregnant for the

**Perseverance is Remembrance**

second time! I needed to get rid of this baby and quick. He couldn't believe it but I must say he took the news much better than he did the first time. Like me, he didn't want to be a father of two; he wasn't even out of school yet and the thought of telling his mother this time was unthinkable. There was no way I was going to jeopardize the newly built relationship with my mom either. I didn't want to bare anymore physical or mental pain. I urged Hakeem to come home immediately; we agreed that we would go to the clinic together to explore our options and that's what we did. I experienced life being sucked out of my helpless body; I felt as if it were my soul leaving my body. Hakeem and I never discussed the topic, ever. I was successful in moving into my new apartment and for once in a long time, I felt independent.

The end of the semester was here and there had been a lot of talk about the NFL draft. My phone was ringing off the hook from people I had known since high school. Of course everyone was curious to know if

**Perseverance is Remembrance**

Hakeem had been signed. I honestly had no idea what he had decided to do. One thing I did know was that he worked really hard and I had been praying him through every step of the way. Hakeem eventually called to tell me which team he signed with. I was happy for him, I had no doubt in my mind that he would've been given an opportunity; he was a great athlete. I thanked God for finding favor over Hakeem and providing him with the tools to succeed. Even though my mom was looking in my best interest before, there was no way Hakeem was going to make it this far and not come through for his child and I was sure of it. I knew only good things came from sacrifice and I figure we both had made some pretty big sacrifices. I knew the tears I shed when I was away had purpose to them.

Hakeem's graduation had come. I knew football training camp was immediately following so I wanted to congratulate him and show my support by attending his graduation ceremony. I wasn't quite sure exactly when it was and apparently that was

**Perseverance is Remembrance**

the plan. I missed the graduation so I wasn't able to let our daughter see her father off. Picking up my daughter from school one day, one of the teachers's asked if I was okay. I asked "Why wouldn't I be?" She went on to say that she knew that I wasn't invited to Hakeem's graduation and instead, along with her family, Ms. Loretta took one of Hakeem's ex-girlfriend's and her son (fathered by another man) to see him. That ball was thrown completely from left field. And it wasn't even the "crazy" girl from before, it was a totally different girl. It was embarrassing to hear from a stranger what had happened. Obviously everyone else knew I wasn't invited except me. I knew Hakeem and I weren't a couple anymore, but silly me; I thought I would've been invited or at least his daughter taken along for the ride. Neither happened, and I was pissed. I called Hakeem to confront him and he swore that he didn't even know the girl was coming; he said it was his mother's idea. My feelings were so hurt. To this very day, Ms. Loretta has never discussed that situation with me. It was then, not when

**Perseverance is Remembrance**

she suggested that several other guys could've been the father of Hakeem's child, not because she didn't pay me a single visit or phone call during my pregnancy, not when she looked me in my eyes and told me not to ask her son for a dime to help support his own child, but that very moment when I smelled an underhanded, conniving, and malicious woman who refuse to take the back seat to any one in Hakeem's life. That hurt for a long time; I eventually let it go.

Since I had adjusted to my civilian job, and my new apartment, I decided it was still something missing from my life. I wanted to pick up where I left off from with school. I successfully completed one full year of community college and earned another year worth of college credits when I was away. I enrolled back in school with the same intentions to earn my psychology degree and this time to finish without anything standing in my way. Days, weeks and months passed by and I hadn't heard from Hakeem. I knew he was trying to adjust to

**Perseverance is Remembrance**

the NFL life but was he that busy? I indulged myself with homework from school and eventually his lack of effort to communicate became unnoticed. The balance between work and school was coming along just fine. I enjoyed the responsibility of being a mommy, learning my way.

Months later, Hakeem called. He wanted to know how things had been going with me and our daughter. I assured him that she was okay. Though there were challenges, I didn't feel like it was anything I couldn't handle. We chatted long enough for me to gather that he was doing quite well for himself. He was fortunate enough to have made the roster and the season was going well. I knew Hakeem had been earning an income, unlike before, and up to that point nothing was offered to me. Completely over the fact that would not be getting back together, I asked Hakeem how he was planning to support his child. Neither I nor Hakeem grew up with our fathers in our lives. We both witnessed our mothers struggle with single parenting, so it

**Perseverance is Remembrance**

was no secret that a child needed either physical and financial support or one versus the other. Since Hakeem couldn't offer the physical part then I was definitely expecting the financial part to relieve some of the stresses I had with work, school, home and a baby. I was practically working two jobs and getting money from my financial aid, so I didn't expect for him to be the primary breadwinner.

I noticed Hakeem lack of interest for the conversation; he asked what was I expecting. I initially asked him for eight hundred dollars a month. I found that to be reasonable enough considering he was averaging over thirty thousand a month. What he didn't know is that I had already been advised by several attorneys. Their take was, they had witnessed cases like mine in the past and solely advised me to get a court order against Hakeem for child support. I knew legally I would be granted five times what I originally asked for but for me it wasn't about the money. I just wanted to feel like I wasn't in this thing alone. I

**Perseverance is Remembrance**

wanted to give Hakeem a fair chance. I had no intentions on quitting either of my jobs or trying to live like a *basketball wife*, so it didn't matter how much money I was promised. Hakeem refused to give me the eight hundred at first. He couldn't understand how I needed eight hundred dollars to support a toddler. I simply said okay. He figured that four hundred sounded better and that would be his final offer. After disputing that figure a few times, I was mentally exhausted and said "Fine"; my mind was made up. Maybe eight hundred was too much. He called back shortly after, to say he would be okay with giving me what I asked for. I was curious to know what changed his mind so fast. He explained that he had been advised by his financial advisor that what I was asking for was considerably reasonable. I was afraid of that. I didn't know if he had a *real* financial advisor or if his mother was advising him. It didn't matter at that point. Hakeem had never done much for his daughter because he was in school and because of that, I tried

**Perseverance is Remembrance**

my best to be understanding. I was utterly insulted by the fact that I was not only his child's mother but his friend first, and I had wanted nothing but the best for him and our child and this was how I was treated; like a thief. I had been taking care of our daughter with my income unaided, and he had the nerve to consult with a total stranger to get proper "advising" on how to take care of his child. It was at that point that I refused his offer.

I saved every dollar, dime and penny I earned from work and school to afford the initial filing fee with an attorney. When I told Hakeem what I was planning he couldn't understand why we couldn't work things out ourselves. I thought we could and I tried. I just didn't want to live a life of having to beg and plead with him or his mother and her malicious antics, to take of our child. I was testing him by giving him a chance to call and present me with any ideas, and he failed. I tested him by allowing him to comply with my offer of eight hundred dollars, and he failed. I saw right then that if I didn't have that "piece of paper," it would forever be a struggle with him and I didn't want to chance it. Hakeem was confident but upset at the same time. He told me that he was the one with the money and that I would need him before he would ever need me. To hear him say that hurt. I had known this guy since I was fourteen years old. We rode the bus together, partied together and prayed together. Were we both really that immature? Hakeem mailed me checks in the amount of four hundred dollars for about five months following that conversation.

The next year was pure hell. I had fallen behind in my bills, trying to afford my lawyers. My school work piled up on me because I didn't have energy to study. I didn't like that Hakeem and I only talked through our attorneys. Every time we had meetings, I had to hear that "Ms. Loretta said this and Ms. Loretta said that." Frankly, I didn't give a damn about what she had to say. Things between her and I had gotten so bad that I would find myself cursing her

**Perseverance is Remembrance**

out. I hated that she under handedly turned Hakeem against me but in the process made me out to be the crazy one. She even insisted that she be present for the visits with Hakeem and our child. We accomplished absolutely nothing except that she truly had a problem. What was the deal with this woman? Why was she being so intrusive? I spent many nights praying to God that he work with my spirit and my patience regarding this matter. It was like I was fighting a complete stranger and we had no respect for one another. That stressful year caused me to have difficulty with keeping up at work. If I wasn't catching up on school work then my nights were spent mostly crying myself to sleep; trying to escape the reality of what my life had become. This was "baby daddy" drama.

While Hakeem and I failed to communicate at all, it didn't stop people from keeping me informed on his success as an NFL player and when he visited home. I lost all interest in knowing anything about him or his family. Of course that didn't last

**Perseverance is Remembrance**

long. I noticed how Ms. Loretta was gradually upgrading herself. Her hair would be fixed every week, nails and toes done. It was when I saw her brand new luxury car that sent me over the edge. I wanted to be happy for her however I just didn't feel like she was genuine. I always found myself angry at her because Hakeem and I relationship had just completely suffered and she was happy. I wanted to scratch, kick and spit on that car, but what good would that have done? Was I jealous? Of course. Was I being selfish? Maybe so. It was even said that she was getting a house built. I felt as if she encouraged his behavior. She made it clear that she was the first lady in Hakeem's life regardless of what was going on, including his child. I refused to sit around and let her get what was rightfully my daughter's, first.

The child support suit lasted for a years. A year of constant arguing, name calling, lies and unnecessary bills amounting to money I didn't have. Finally, after endless arguments and sleepless nights, our case was settled right before it went to trial. I was awarded more child support than I initially asked for, and we were both granted joint custody. At first, this decision didn't sit well with me at all. I wondered how the hell that would work. After a while I didn't care. I grew excited knowing that I would be relieved every week during the off season, every summer, and some weekends during the season. I planned more time for work and school and a chance to get out and make some friends. Even after the case ended, Ms. Loretta continued to over step her boundaries as just the grandmother. Her and I still didn't get along like we should have and when we did it was phony. She, on several occasions, refrained from calling or coming to see her grandchild when Hakeem and I didn't get along. When she wanted to be, she was a huge help to me but I was use to her disappearing acts.

As time went on, Hakeem and I agreed to handle things more civil amongst ourselves, especially after he admitted to the added drama his mother caused by in-

**Perseverance is Remembrance**

truding. We had no reason to fight now, he was paying child support and he could have his child anytime he wanted. I looked forward to my relief. I was more focused on graduating than ever. We actually became close and comfortable enough to discuss other aspects of our lives. It was no secret that we both dated other people. We gave each other helpful hints on how to have successful relationships. It was nice for the moment.

# 6
## ~Baseball Season~

Off season was here and it was Hakeem's turn to get our daughter for the weekend. It was a Friday night and I wanted to get out. I had heard several radio ads for a club called "The Loft"; I decided to go there. I didn't have many friends at home at the time so I went alone. I figured going out would give me a chance to meet new people.

A *white button up* shirt and a pair of little black shorts was the perfect outfit to show off the compliments of how the army had sculpted my body. Though my clothes were cute, it was the four inch heels that did the trick. Sipping on *whatever was clever* that night and trying to maneuver throughout the crowd was crazy. It was damn crowded in there, but I'm glad I stepped out.

**Perseverance of Remembrance**

He and his friends had been *popping bottles* and swaying from side to side the whole night. I could tell they were celebrating something, just couldn't tell what. He was tall; with smooth caramel skin, and with dimples that looked liked they hurt as they pierced the side of his face. He wore his hair low and that I liked. He too, had on a *white collared shirt* that complimented his skin tone and jeans that gripped his butt flawlessly. I kept my cool as I got closer to him and his friends but I just kept saying to myself "Oh my God!" He was just that gorgeous to me. I walked passed them so that I could get in line to take a picture. Honey, when I say I strutted like I was on "Rip the Runway," I was working it with those four inches. After taking my picture, I turned to walk away and instead of my dimple crush, it was one of his friends that grabbed me to take a picture with of all them. "Damn," I said to myself. I guessed that was good enough, it got me on the field. They were all gentlemen and seemed really nice; older than I was, but it didn't

**Perseverance of Remembrance**

matter.

My attraction for older men trumped my attraction for the younger ones. A few of them complimented me on how beautiful I was and while that was nice and all, I still had my eye on that caramel prize. I winked, thanked them all and moved right along. As I walked away, I noticed my crush walking along side of me; he followed me all the way to the bar. Subsequent to him buying me a drink, we introduced ourselves to one another; I will call him Carlos. We chatted for the rest of then evening over drinks and appetizers. We concluded by dirtying up the dance floor with some of R. Kelly's old slide remixes. Though he asked for my number, it was my email address he seemed to be more interested in. That was the first!

Carlos explained that he and his friends were out celebrating his last night in the States. He was a baseball player and he was headed to Italy for some training. He wanted to keep in touch and while he promised to call sometimes, it would be

**Perseverance is Remembrance**

email that he would mostly communicate through until he got back. I thought that was cool. We talked just about every day.

We learned a lot about each other during that time. He had a sense of humor and I loved that. I looked forward to his return. When Carlos got back, he called and we met up. That became our routine; we would hang out, talk, party and just kick back and chill. We enjoyed each others company. I didn't want anything from him; just hanging out with him was good enough for me. He had a son around the same age as my daughter and so sometimes we would get them together to take them out. It was weird because we knew some of the same people; I guess I wondered why we had never bumped into each other. The mystery of Carlos, sexually, kept me attracted to him but once that mystery was over so was my attraction. The sex was *okay*; I didn't hold it against him, I just figured we were meant to be *just* friends. Carlos and I continued to hang out and we talked often. He continued to come in and out of town for work. I knew Carlos' mother had been sick. He would fall into these depressed moods because he knew that she was soon to die. I felt for him; never had I experienced the death of one of my parents but I knew he was hurting. I did what any friend would do. I gave him time when he needed it, but mostly I was there to console him and to keep his mind off the pain. After his mother's death, Carlos revealed to me that he was actually married. "Excuse me?" What else was I supposed to say? I didn't even know how to respond. I had never seen a ring on this man's finger, we stayed out late numerous times and we were *just* friends. Why did he feel the need to keep that from me? I knew he had been grieving but I did let him know that I was very upset with him. I wanted to know more.

Carlos was still married to his son's mother and had been for about four years. He said they both mutually agreed that a divorce would be best for them both; however they procrastinated on signing the papers so they just considered themselves

**Perseverance is Remembrance**

"separated." I didn't give a damn! My mom told me a married man is a married man regardless of his situation. If he doesn't have those papers, then keep it moving. What had I done? This was the second married man I had slept with but I knew nothing about their wives from the start. Did that count for anything?

By that point, I didn't feel bad about not liking Carlos' sex game. At first, I felt shallow, but certainly not now. Carlos and I got over that hump and agreed that since we were just friends, from that point on, no more lies. While he never got over his mother's death, he felt better about it. I still viewed Carlos as a friend and therefore we still saw each other quite often when he wasn't playing baseball. I can remember a while back we went to the mall to do some shopping; well I was just along for the ride. Carlos was shopping for a wedding gift and I was there for support. Walking past this store, I saw this beautiful dress in the window. It was an olive green and yellow color, with long, flowing layers. It was gorgeous. He told me to get the dress but I declined his offer and dreamed about it later.

Valentine's Day had come. My ritual involved exchanging gifts with my daughter so while I was out shopping for her a perfect gift, Carlos called me. He asked me to meet him at a gas station; one near a highway because he was on his way to Chicago for the weekend. I did just that. When I arrived, I saw his car and he signaled for me to drive over while he ran in to pay for gas. When he came back he said he just wanted to say bye before he went to Chicago. He reached in his trunk and out he pulled the stunning dress from the mall. I was so surprised and happy at the same time. I didn't know if I should have accepted such a pricey gift, but I did and Happy Valentine's Day to me! I gave him a hug and wished for his safe return. My daughter and I enjoyed a wonderful weekend; she loved her gifts and I loved the cartoon coloring book she gave me. It was funny that every gift she gave me was

**Perseverance is Remembrance**

always something she really wanted. It was her way of knowing I would be giving it back.

By the end of the weekend, it was time to get my mind back into work and school mode. While I was cleaning the house, I received a phone call from a woman and I didn't recognize the number. When I answered, she asked me if I knew who she was. Suddenly, I had a flash back. I replied "No, but you clearly know who I am." She must have heard the aggravation in my tone and she quickly apologized. As the conversation progressed, I learned that she was claiming to be Carlos' girlfriend, who lived in Chicago. She believed we were having an affair. She said she had read all of our text messages and emails to and from one another and though there was nothing sexual detailed in our dialog, she didn't understand why we spoke so frequently. She claimed that as we spoke, she was looking at a naked picture of someone in Carlos' phone. My first question to her was "Where is he?" He was in the

**Perseverance is Remembrance**

other room sleeping while she was up playing inspector gadget. I didn't blame her for being suspicious of her man, simply because he lied to me and we were just friends. What I didn't agree with was that she felt it her right to be going through this man's phone. No relationship should consist of invasion of privacy. But at the same time, I wasn't his wife so I didn't really know the lengths that marriages went through.

    I quickly let her know my position with Carlos and while she wasn't convinced, I revealed to her that when we first met, I wasn't aware of his marriage so yes, we slept together but after that, we have been nothing less nor more than just friends ever since. As soon as I mentioned how well our kids played together, she insisted that I go no further. She said that first of all, Carlos was her boyfriend; not her husband and that he didn't have kids. Now I was confused. I was starting to think this woman had the wrong number. She had no idea that her boyfriend was actually married with a son. So it wasn't me after all she needed

**Perseverance is Remembrance**

to be worried about, it was his wife! I felt bad for her as she cried for an hour on the other end of my phone. I encouraged her to talk to Carlos before she made anymore calls; it was him who had lied to her, not random women. I particularly was upset with Carlos because along with telling me he was married he should've told me he had a girlfriend too. I hadn't caught feelings for him or anything, which would've just been fatal for him. I was more disappointed that he didn't respect our friendship enough to be honest with me. A few weeks had passed and I hadn't heard from him. That let me know he knew about the conversation I had with his girlfriend; perhaps he felt guilty and embarrassed. Carlos portrayed himself as if he was a man, yet he didn't act like one. He was a liar and I didn't want a friend like that so we never spoke again.

# 7
## ~Falling Was Easy, It Was Getting Back Up That Was Hard~

It was at the end of my work shift when I saw him. I looked right through him though; I was exhausted and it was already three in the morning. The Dj was playing some classic slow jams and giving shouts out on the mic. A friend of mine, Olivia, had referred me to an easy weekend job printing pictures for a photographer at a club.

He and his friends had just been pushed out of the back door by my favorite bouncer, Lawrence. I thanked Lawrence every time he did his job. It wasn't uncommon for guys to linger around after the club shut down, especially the heavily intoxicated ones; Lawrence knew I hated it. I went to the restroom to wash my hands

**Perseverance is Remembrance**

from all of the nasty ass money I had handled throughout the night. It was disgusting witnessing girls pull money from their soggy panties as if it were a magic trick. When I got back to my work station to gather my belongings, there that same guy was, peeping through and knocking on the back door.

    I took a deep breath, rolled my eyes and opened the door. Lawrence came running to my defense but after throwing my hand up in the air, he slowed down a little. The guy said he had forgotten something inside, so I let him back in to retrieve it. As I grabbed my purse and turned around, he was standing less than two feet behind me. He said he had forgotten to get my number. Even though I was tired and was potentially suffering from a mild heart attack from the second hand smoke that night, I laughed. He caught me off guard. At that point, I signaled for Lawrence to come back over to escort him out again. The next two weeks were the same. I admired his persistence. Essentially,

**Perseverance is Remembrance**

I thought he was handsome; I just didn't want to be bothered. I eventually gave in to him and asked that he not come up there any more bothering me. Tony was very tall, a lot thinner than I preferred, with beautiful brown skin and he dressed very nice. I hadn't seen him around town, before he stalked me that is. Our town was small enough to run into the same people all the time even if you didn't know them. Tony said he was originally from New York, and moved around several times before coming here, which I thought, explained why I hadn't noticed him before.

We went out a few times and he seemed cool; a little weird, but cool. At the start of us getting to know one another we both bared to each other that neither of us wanted a commitment. Somewhere down the line, our lines of communication had crossed because I found myself in a relationship with him. I realized that I was feeling and doing things only my mate would push me to do. Tony was the only child and his parents lived in a small town

**Perseverance is Remembrance**

about two hours east of where we were. He insisted that after a few months of seeing each other that I meet his parents. I, of course, wasn't too happy about that. I just had developed this *thing* about parents. Luckily, his mother and father were beautiful people; they reminded me of the Cosby's. I was delighted to see him and his mother interact with one another. It wasn't a freakishly close relationship; like she had control over him. I loved how his father still opened the doors for his mother and pulled out her chairs. Overall it seemed as if they were still in love and that Tony grew up in a well rounded home.

Tony eventually ignored the fact that I didn't want him showing up at my weekend job. He would pop up out no where, even after he promised he had other things to do for the evening. I became extremely annoyed because I felt like I was being watched or like he was my body guard. After a while I noticed Tony got aggravated at the sight of guys talking to me. He made it clear to everyone that I was his woman

**Perseverance is Remembrance**

and his only. His aggravation went from possession to anger. Some people even advised me not to date him because they were sure that he was dating other girls at the same time. Fortunately, I had never had any run-in's with those other women, which wasn't likely; the other woman always had a way of finding me. Plus, I figured they couldn't have been happy with him. Tony spent most of his time in my face tracking my every move. Over the course of our "relationship," Tony *advised* me on who I should and shouldn't talk to. It was like he didn't even respect the time I spent with my own child. This was a lot coming from a man I wasn't even sleeping with and didn't plan to.

Although technically, I was a single woman, I noticed the lies I was telling Tony, just to get form underneath his watchful eye. I was being sneaky for no apparent reason. What kept me from telling this guy to lose my number? I didn't know but I needed a break. Olivia asked me to go out with her for drinks. The funny thing is that

**Perseverance is Remembrance**

Olivia didn't drink. So what the hell was really going on? She had also been going through the ringer with her daughter's father, which I understood and was one of the reasons we became really good friends; for support. Her situation was a little different than mine; I advised her to leave him; he was no good for. She was a beautiful girl with a gorgeous daughter; she had much more to offer. Anyway, she took my advice and decided to go out with a nice young man she had met. She wanted me to go with her so that it didn't look like a date. I did. She had come up with a random excuse for Tony so that he wouldn't be looking for me.

It felt so good to be out with my girl; she was always a joy to be around. We arrived at a night club on the central west end of town. It was small but elegant; I liked it. Olivia and I went straight to the bar. While we waited for her friend to arrive, she begged me not to laugh when I saw him. I had never seen him before and I guess she figured I wouldn't approve of his

**Perseverance is Remembrance**

look. We always made fun of each others crushes. When I saw him, I was caught off guard. It was just his funny *Freddy Krueger* sweater that tickled my giggled box. Aside from the fact that he was much shorter than her, nothing major, he was a really nice guy. He seemed fanatical over Olivia, and it's always nice to have someone who treats you well. He was actually pretty awesome because he had brought along a friend to entertain me.

    Jimmy was a professional basketball player for Dallas. I honestly didn't care who he was or what he did for a living, it was just nice to be in the presence of someone other than Tony, who by the way could've been somewhere close spying on my every move. Jimmy wasn't really a "looker" but he had a great personality and sense of humor. Plus he paid for my drinks and offered exceptional conversation for the rest of the evening. As the night came to an end, Jimmy decided he wanted to be the one to take me home; it gave us a chance to talk more, without the loud music. I figured he

**Perseverance is Remembrance**

was harmless, so I allowed him to take me home. Tony hadn't called my phone all night so he must have been out with his friends, his other girlfriends, or at home. Nevertheless, I was happy he hadn't been blowing my phone up. Jimmy and I discussed our likes and dislikes, our favorite foods and things to do. I told him that I did have a child and after finding out that Hakeem was the father, he said he knew him; they weren't friends but they knew *of* each other. Upon my arrival to my apartment, we exchanged numbers and ended the night with a friendly hug. We planned to keep in touch with one another and we did just that.

Walking through the door that night was like a sigh of relief. My feet were throbbing from another pair of my famous four inch heels; I just wanted them off. Not even five minutes later did my phone ring with a text message from Tony, asking how my night was. I replied by saying "good." I told him I was headed to bed and that I would probably talk to him the next day. He wanted to come over and asked that I stay up until he got there. As much as I didn't want to be bothered with him, I said okay anyway. I flew through the house pulling off my dress and washed my face from the makeup. Soon after, he was knocking at my door. I found it really strange that he had gotten there so quickly because he lived about twenty-five minutes away from me.

Once I answered the door and securely locked it behind me, I turned around, his fist, with full force, struck the side of my face; leaving me no choice but to fall to the floor. How dumb of me to think he was out minding his own business. He had been parked near my house the entire time, witnessing Jimmy dropping me off. I had never been hit by a man before and for the first time, I felt physically helpless. As I guarded my face, he continued to kick me in my back, forcing me to stay on the floor. He was furious that I had the nerve to make him look foolish by being seen with another guy. While every inch of me wanted to get up and thrust into him, I was just too weak to do so.

**Perseverance is Remembrance**

The next morning, I had a swollen face. I quickly called my mom to give her some excuse as to why I couldn't pick up my daughter. I needed time for my face to heal. I couldn't believe what happened the night before, but when I saw the card Tony had left, it became a reality. The card read how sorry he was and that he wasn't sure what came over him. He pleaded that I never hurt him like that again. I was overwhelmed. I didn't even love this guy, let alone like him enough for him to treat me this way. Tony called a few times after that and I refused all calls. I never told a soul because I was sure it wouldn't happen again.

Jimmy and I talked much more. He would take me out to eat, to movies, and we even had game night with some of his friends. Jimmy wasn't demanding in any way and I was relieved. Neither of us was ready for anything serious and we were honest with one another. I knew Jimmy would be leaving soon going to Georgia for

**Perseverance is Remembrance**

some basketball training; he asked if I would join him. I knew if Tony found that out he would've guaranteed my misery, so I decided to continue not to answer any of his calls. I just wanted to be away from him; far, far away. I had a great time with Jimmy. He was my personal tour guide; he showed me around to all of the hottest clubs, I met some really cool people and he spoiled me with shopping. He treated me like a queen. Tony's calls became more frequent while I was gone but still, I didn't answer a single one. Coming home was the hard part; I knew I had to. I didn't want to put up with anymore of Tony's shit.

Another weekend came and it was time for me to work at the club. It was crowded as usual and Olivia and I *people watched* and laughed at the comedy that consumed the club that night. We usually allowed each other to take breaks during our slow periods, which were seldom, however this night I did not want to take any chances on running into Tony on the dance floor or back by the restrooms. It was almost the end of

**Perseverance is Remembrance**

the night when he text my phone and asked me to swing by his house. He hadn't seen me since he beat the shit out of me. Although I was skeptical, I decided to go anyway; I had previously left clothes and shoes at his house and I wanted my stuff back. I told him I would be right over.

    Club hours were over and it was time to go. I ran into a guy by the name of Corey as I was packing my things up to leave. I'd seen him around the club before; he had even tried to get with me but I would always tell him I had a boyfriend. Anyway, he kept me company as I cleaned and while doing so, my phone rang. Tony's picture popped up on the face of my phone and Corey asked me how I knew him. I just shrugged with a funky look on my face. Then he goes on to ask me if I lived in the Chase. The Chase Park Plaza condos were valued at no less than a half million dollars. I said "No." He said he knew Tony and he's also hung out with him before and that's how he knew his girlfriend lived in the Chase. I saw nothing but red. This man had the audacity, not only to date me, but to

**Perseverance is Remembrance**

put his hands on me and drive me through hell while he dated a woman that was damn near rich? Corey asked that I not act crazy with Tony however he didn't care if I told him about our conversation. Corey and I exchanged numbers and he talked to me as I made my way over to Tony's house.

When I walked through his front door, I had Corey on speaker phone so that Tony could hear. He threw a huge fit as to why I was even talking to him. I simply asked him if he had a girlfriend; he said no. Honestly, I didn't care and didn't want to flatter him by thinking I did. I grabbed my things and walked out of the door. I would've run to my car but I still had on my little black dress and my heels so I didn't want to fall. Tony was furious; he chased me and by time he caught up to me, I was at my car. He basically said we had been through too much to be allowing other people to mess up a good thing. He grabbed my phone and called Corey. They argued and Tony tried to convince me that Corey was lying, but Corey was sure of what he knew, and I

**Perseverance is Remembrance**

believed him. I fought for him to give me the phone back but after hanging up on Corey, he threw my phone down the sewer. As pissed as I was, I didn't care about that damn phone, I just wanted to get in my car and drive away. While he begged me not believe the lies, I continued to pursue the entry of my car. Tony then grabbed me by the neck, turned me around and slammed me against my car. He punched me several times in my face and when I dropped to the ground he kicked me over and over again. I knew this was it for me.

It was almost four in the morning, no one was out at this time, and my phone had been thrown in a sewer; I couldn't even make an emergency call. I didn't need a mirror to see that, once again, my face was a mess. Tony threw my car keys on the ground and he walked away, leaving me there. I felt the warm blood from my nose run from my face and watched as it drained in the same sewer my phone had been thrown. I was able to pick myself up once again and drive home.

**Perseverance is Remembrance**

I was a victim of what most would describe as *domestic abuse*. I was too embarrassed to say anything to anyone and therefore have kept it a secret until now. Falling on the ground was much easier than rising up again.

## 8
## ~His Secrets; My Lies

Some guys feared dating me. Hakeem had his way of subliminally scaring them off and making it seem like it had nothing to do with me at all.

I can remember becoming good friends with this guy. We had actually known each other for some years before we began to see each other often. We would talk and see one another just about every other day. Being that Hakeem and I lived in different cities, I wasn't totally sure how he would always know what I was up to. He somehow found out about this particular guy and took it upon himself to contact him. I wondered why I hadn't talked to him for about a week; he forwarded me the message he was sent and I couldn't believe my eyes, especially since Hakeem and I hadn't dated in years. Why was he concerned with who I was with? He claimed he was more worried

**Perseverance is Remembrance**

about the welfare of his child. Now, had that truly been the reason, I wouldn't have blown up at him. I understood from a more general point of view where Hakeem was coming from. Could you imagine how tragic things would've been if Tony and I ended up married? My dating life sucked; I dated men who lied about having girlfriends and wives, guys who cheated and beat on me. Just when I thought things couldn't get any worse, I met Nate.

One day I ran across an old friend; my very first crush from middle school. I can remember over ten years ago when Nate walked into the classroom, it was love at first sight. Ten years later, nothing changed. I don't know what made me look for him, but initially we talked over *Myspace*; another one of those social networks. A mutual friend of ours discouraged me from developing any new feelings for him. She didn't say exactly why except for she had heard some rumors throughout the years. That wasn't good enough for me; I understood she didn't want me to get my

**Perseverance is Remembrance**

feelings hurt but I figured "What else could go wrong?" You see, I left the school district before my eighth grade year was over. My mom wasn't happy with my progress; she put me back into private school so that was the last time I had ever seen Nate. Like the rest of my middle school friends, Nate too, went on to experience high school without me. I was confused by what kind of rumors she had heard, but I was willing to take a chance. My past, I'm sure was far worse. As long as he didn't smack me around, I was winning.

    Nate was excited to hear from me. Our first date was simple. I remembered seeing him for the first time in years and he looked exactly the same except for with longer hair. He was always a clean cut kind of guy, red bone, with the darkest features I had ever seen on a guy. He took one look at me and stared pretty much the entire evening. He said I looked the same to him. He was impressed with my natural curvy body; he made fun of how skinny and awkward I looked back then. We took advantage of the whole night to get caught up on what was going on in each other's lives. I was quite shocked to hear that Nate was diagnosed with diabetes at the age of thirteen; this was right after I left school. Fortunately, he said he had complete control over his illness. After some near fatal events occurred, he became more serious about his health.

Of course, I snuck my way into his dating life. He said he hadn't dated in a long while. I wanted to know why this gorgeous, "no kids" having, never married man didn't have a girlfriend. He seemed completely normal. Nate was surprised that I was in the military. All he remembered was me as this frail, tom boy, that was timid and bashful. He couldn't imagine the thought of me ordering anybody around. And even though I showed him pictures of my daughter, he didn't believe it. He remembered me being one of the only girls back then who never dreamed of having kids. Nate and I talked for the rest of the evening, I was happy to know his family was doing well. He seemed happy with life and it made me much

**Perseverance is Remembrance**

happier that we were back in touch after all those years.

Since date number one was a success, we decided to go out again. Each moment we were together from then on was phenomenal. We had genuine fun together. We had so much in common yet we were so different. Our spontaneous dates turned into spending every other day together. If we weren't at work, then we were in each other's faces. Nate grew to be my best friend. He was easier to talk to than any friend I had ever had. He never judged me, and he actually listened when I spoke. He was always available for me and was very compassionate. Ironically we had been much closer than either of us realized. We resided in the same apartment community that I had recently moved to. He hadn't been there very long. We grew fond of each other in a short period of time. We spent most of our nights talking, and catching up on things I thought we missed.

There was something about Nate, and though I felt it in my gut, I looked past it. I

**Perseverance is Remembrance**

wanted him so badly to be the one for me that I was willing to be blinded by the obvious. Nate introduced me to his entire family and though I didn't feel comfortable, they loved me and I felt the same about them. I didn't move as quickly with the "family" thing. I vowed never to bring another guy home since Hakeem; not unless he was going to be my husband for sure. In addition, I knew Hakeem would still be around and critical with anyone I showed interest. Most guys didn't get that but Nate understood and he wasn't offended. He was patient with me when it came to a lot of things, including sex. I told him in the beginning that I wasn't looking for anything sexual too soon but we were in our fourth month of dating and hadn't even kissed yet. I was running out of conversations to have with him. Unlike Carlos, I actually saw a future for Nate and I; I wanted to share that level of intimacy with him. At the time, he was everything I wanted in a man, well mostly.

**Perseverance is Remembrance**

Our first holiday was approaching, Valentine's Day. Nate wouldn't tell me what he had planned for me; all I knew was that I had to be clear of my apartment that entire day. I was so excited not to be getting *just* a coloring book as a gift! Later on that night he called me to come home. Walking through my front door was like walking into an enchanted forest. He transformed my apartment into this romantic, candlelit paradise; smothered in elegant rose pedals with my favorite artist, Brian McKnight, serenading me in the background.

I was overwhelmed but flattered that someone thought I was special enough to take out the time to make me smile. My dining room table was layered in seafood, my food of abundance. He was nervous, since he prepared the meal himself. There was absolutely nothing he had to be nervous about because everything was wonderful. There were jumbo sized, chocolate covered strawberries located on my coffee table. Last, but certainly not

**Perseverance is Remembrance**

least, he escorted me upstairs to my bedroom, where a ring box sat comfortably in the middle of my bed, which was also layered in rose pedals. Nate seemed way more nervous than I did; I just prayed this wasn't a proposal. He held my hand in his sweaty and trembling palms and recited to me that he loved me. He vowed that as long as I allowed him to be apart of my life, he would never hurt me. I felt so special when he slid that ring on my finger. No, we weren't engaged but his sweet words were everything I imagined my husband to recite. After all of the gift exchanges, we headed over to his mother's house so that I could flaunt my new ring, not to mention the heart shaped, diamond necklace he put around my neck.

We later made our way back to my apartment, got everything cleaned up and headed to bed. I had sex on the brain. I mean, it was Valentine's Day; cliché but it was perfect for our first time. My probation period was over and it was time for us to get it on. I sprayed my finest perfume,

**Perseverance is Remembrance**

Victoria Secret's "Very Sexy Now!" I put on a pair of my cheekiest boy shorts and I backed my ass up on him as subtle as I could, but nothing worked. I eventually got up to take a cold shower soon after I saw we weren't getting anywhere. And no, cold showers do not work; they just leave you angry and *cold*. Despite the flaw in that romantic night of no romance, it was still a good night. However, I noticed that every night after that ended the same damn way. I started to become discouraged and believed that Nate just wasn't attracted to me like I was attracted to him. It bothered me so I decided to talk to him about it. He assured me that he was very much attracted to me but he had no intentions on rushing me into bed. He thought highly of me and said I was the woman he truly loved. I must say, that worked for a long time, until I began to assume other stuff.

I managed to get an appointment with my *celebrity* hairstylist, Antoine. He moved to Los Angeles to pursue his dream, but came back once a month to cater to his

**Perseverance is Remembrance**

special clients. It was difficult getting an appointment with him, so when he scheduled me for a Saturday morning, I got right up and flew down to his shop. Nate and I had plans that night to attend one of the hottest parties and I had to be flawless. I hadn't saw Antoine in months, even though we would text, it was good to be sitting in his chair; pouring out my heart to him. He was more of a counselor to me than anything.

While he worked his magic on my head, he wanted to know more about this new found love of mine. I had never told Antoine Nate's name but I described him as best I could. As Antoine tracked my weave, Nate called to see how I was coming along. My phone rested on Antoine's work station, and when he saw Nate's picture, I noticed his body language changed. He questioned me about Nate, all of which, I had none of the answers which was weird because we spent long nights getting to know one another. Deep down inside, I knew where he was going with it. Antoine told me he was cool

**Perseverance is Remembrance**

with the same circle of friends as Nate, some of which who knew him much better than I pretended, and advised me to be careful. He made a call to one of the friends and placed his phone on speaker. I was very upset leaving the shop that day but decided not to let it ruin our plans for that evening. Antoine reassured me that his intent wasn't to upset me however he felt as if I hadn't properly been counseled about Nate and since we were friends, he did so.

It was time to head to the party, and Nate and I stepped out impeccably fashionable. Physically, we complimented each other perfectly. I tried my best to have a good time but Antoine's and my conversation earlier that day was in the back of my mind. Nate noticed something was different about me; he said I was acting *spacey*. After the party was over, we headed back to my apartment. I was too tired to discuss what was bothering me; I really didn't know how to bring it to him and so I needed time to think about it. As we lay

**Perseverance is Remembrance**

in the bed, Nate asked me if I wanted to talk about it, I said "No" and went to sleep. As time went on, I found myself starting several conversations that gave him the *okay* to tell me what it was I figured he needed to tell me but never would. That must have been why he broke out in that uncomfortable sweat on Valentine's Day.

Weeks passed and I decided it was time for a vacation. I had been non-stop at work and school and I wanted sometime to relax. I planned a trip to Florida for Nate and me. He was amazed because he had never been before so he was as excited about the trip as I was. Suddenly, things between Nate and I got tense. There was no way for him to ignore the rumors any longer. It was scary because at this point not only did he hear them but he knew they were loud enough for me to hear as well. I just couldn't nail exactly what the problem was, or at least, that's what I kept telling myself; I didn't want to face it. It was hard hearing that the man I grew to love was no good for me. Nate loved me, he treated me with the

**Perseverance is Remembrance**

utmost respect, and he showered me with gifts and gave me the undivided attention I deserved. I didn't want to believe the stories about him, but it did explain an awful lot. Nate knew that I knew he wasn't being honest with me. I wanted to let him know the kind of woman I really was; giving him a chance to talk to me about anything. That's why it was so important for me to build a friendship with a person before anything else. During times of hardships it's always more comforting to know that you have a friend before a mate. With all of the opportunities I had given Nate to come to me first, it was my turn to go to him.

The next day at work I was totally distracted. I knew today would be the day that I confronted Nate with my suspicions. My head was filled with memories of the sexless nights, excuses, and not to mention the warnings. As soon as I was able to take my first break, I grabbed my phone and text Nate and asked him something I was sure would change our relationship, for good. If it wasn't true, he would more than

**Perseverance is Remembrance**

likely hate me. But how was I to ignore the feminine circle of friends he had, his roommate who I'm sure was a man but wore girl clothes. There were copious times where his own friends had mistakenly called him "girl" during casual conversation. And how could I count out his *over the top* flamboyant mannerisms? I worked up the courage to ask him if he'd ever date men before. His reply was "What made you ask me that?" Wow! I couldn't believe he answered like that. I cried and soon after left work; I could no longer concentrate. Its one thing when you *think* you know something, it's another thing when you *know* it to be true. I didn't talk to Nate for the rest of the day. When he text and called me, I ignored him.

There were so many mixed emotions I was feeling; I just didn't want to say anything to him I would regret. Besides, he still hadn't really said much. I felt like a complete idiot; a fool that paraded around town; around his family and friends like I had won a grand prize. There was no way

**Perseverance is Remembrance**

his family knew about this, wouldn't someone have slipped me a note or something? I felt like ultimately, it was my fault. A woman's intuition never lies. The signs are almost always there. I noticed the way other men looked at him; the way he looked at other men. I saw that his eyebrows were more perfect than mine. I knew that before we went out, he needed to try on every outfit in his closet. I saw the way he *whipped his hair* on the dance floor in the club. I even noticed how he smacked his lips when he ate and talked. I saw all of these things from day one and I still ignored them. I wanted so badly to give him the benefit of the doubt; after all, he was my friend first. I didn't know what to say to him once I saw him again.

Nate was nervous about speaking to me but he knew it was something he had to do. I cried as he apologized and tried to make sense of this mess. If anything, I felt more sorrow for him. Why should anyone have to live a double life on account of what other's think of them? I couldn't imagine what he was going through all of this time, even before I came along. What other lies had he told? How many women had he hurt? Did he even like women? And most important to me, how many guys had he been sexually active with? Was it safe?

Nate confirmed that he was in the past sexual with the guys he dated. The vision of his skinny body bent over for another muscular male body climbing on his back disturbed me and it made me feel sick to my stomach. I was in love with a *gay man*. He explained that because of his past, he wasn't too eager to hop into bed with me; I respected him for that. I just couldn't understand the point of our relationship. Truthfully, I wasn't into to investigating a guy's past, unless it posed a health risk and this was definitely fatal for me. So many more questions came about. Was he the top or bottom? Did he perform oral sex? Did he receive? I was afraid the more he told me, the more I would want to know and the

**Perseverance is Remembrance**

more I was going to hurt and come closer to fainting.

As tears streamed down his face and mine, he told me that ever since middle school, he was teased about the way he talked, the way he held his hands, even the way he stood. He figured that people saw something in him that he was afraid to see in himself and because of that he grew curious. He was so sure that his past was behind him and that his future was with the woman he loved; his wife and their children. He wanted *normal love*. For some strange reason, I stayed with Nate. I convinced myself that a "once" gay man could live a normal heterosexual lifestyle if that's what he truly wanted to do.

As time went on, I found myself embarrassed to be with Nate. I would defend him; lie to people when they asked about him. I was even dishonest to my family. I remember going to the hospital for a terrible accident my mom was involved in and while everyone's health should've been my main focus, it was how my family would view Nate after meeting him. He was no secret. My mom was certain that when she met him, I had to be kidding. My friends laughed at me and thought I was losing my mind. I didn't want Nate to think I was typical, and therefore I didn't ridicule and curse him for mistakes he felt like he made in the past. I wanted him to know that although he deceived me, I was genuine about the person I'd shown him; I was loyal, honest and humble. I wasn't one to judge anyone anymore for anything especially after some of the choices I had made in the past. I still sought Nate's approval. Ultimately, Nate just revealed to me his deepest, darkest secret and I wanted to be the one to help him through his pain.

We resumed our vacation plans to Florida and for the most part we enjoyed ourselves. We partied, shopped, tanned on the sunny beaches and ate our hearts out. Breathing that southern air was so refreshing and I wanted to use that as inspiration for Nate and me to start over. I must admit, it was easier for me to walk

**Perseverance is Remembrance**

around oblivious, than knowing my man had previously been pounded on by another grown ass man. This was truly a test of my will. As it got closer to the end of our trip, something happened; I'm not sure what it was. We literally, stopped talking to one another.

Nate decided that our last night in Florida, he would go out by himself. I started to come to the conclusion that this whole nightmare was bigger than me. I wasn't as strong as I thought and I didn't want to be; not for this. We packed our things when he returned and we went home. Weeks passed after the trip ended before we spoke again. Aside from him checking on me, there was nothing more. Our relationship had taken a turn for the worse and considering the circumstances, I was hurt, but I didn't care anymore. We eventually came to a mutual agreement that the best thing was to end our relationship. He argued with me relentlessly and constantly made excuses for not being able to give any of my personal belongings back.

**Perseverance is Remembrance**

I had already made my mind up that I would return him the ring and necklace; I didn't want any part of him. I didn't want the pictures we had taken throughout the course of our relationship either, so I told him to take out the memory card in the camera we shared and I would take the camera. Nate didn't expect that I would be giving him the jewelry back, and I think that hurt him the most. I left and although I struggled with not calling, I stayed away.

Weeks after our break up blew over; I was still sad but I tried my best to be in high spirits. A friend of mine Michelle called to check on me just about everyday. She witnessed the love Nate and I shared with one another and couldn't believe we had broken up. I never told her any of my suspicions about him, so she had no idea. Michelle came over one day to go walking with me. While she waited for me to get some clothes on, we talked about my trip to Florida. She had never been and wanted to see the pictures. I told her that I gave the pictures to Nate, I just had the camera. I

**Perseverance is Remembrance**

had already purchased a new memory card so when I grabbed the camera to replace the old one, there it was, the pictures I told Nate to take out. I tossed Michelle the camera and told her to take a look; I guess he didn't want the pictures either. Moments later, I heard a scream. Michelle ran to me and directed the camera to my face. All I could is cry. There were pictures of Nate kissing men. The thing that startled me was the pictures were taken after our trip. In the pictures I noticed Nate had on the clothes I bought him on the trip.

"You have to be fucking kidding me" was what Michelle said. She thought it was a joke. I had no choice but to be completely honest with her as to why we actually broke up. I felt little and less than nothing because I allowed my heart to be broken by a gay man. I must have been desperate. I called Nate immediately, but all of the cursing and insults I made towards him did no good. I threatened to tell his mother, but I figured I wouldn't be telling her anything she and the rest of his family didn't already

**Perseverance is Remembrance**

know. I was the only blind one in this equation. I later found out Nate was secretly having a relationship with some guy. Turns out he didn't have regard for anyone's feelings and cared for only himself. He even began to date another girl after me, but that was a total fail. While she thought I was playing the role of the "jealous ex-girlfriend," I could really care less about Nate. I slipped her the note I wished someone had slipped me. It was hard redeeming me from that nightmare. Many would say I was stupid for even considering a relationship after hearing rumors about him. While I saw a genuinely, good person, Nate was also selfish; he was a habitual liar and he was not happy with himself; therefore it was hard for him to be happy with anyone else. The tale of the *down low* brother had become my reality.

# 9
## ~Four Walls~

My civilian job consisted of me working in a dirty warehouse. I operated heavy machinery, loaded and unloaded trailer's, shipped and received important merchandise for customers and put up with the endless bullshit threw my way from management. I was the only woman in my department working with thirty men.

The average customer was a middle age to older male. We serviced construction workers, electricians, plumbers; name it, we supplied it. When they saw me for the first time, they thought they were on candid camera. I guess seeing a beautiful woman in their line of work was uncommon. It was hilarious to see some of the reactions I got; even a few of my managers enjoyed them. These men did not think I was capable of doing the job but after I proved them wrong, and we built great relationships with

**Perseverance is Remembrance**

one another, most of them grew as my mentors, some even close friends. A lot of them felt more comfortable with me helping them and looked forward to seeing me. Some even spent long periods of time at the loading docks and walking around the warehouse entertaining me while I worked. A lot of them spent more money than what was planned! A few of the guys personally delivered lunch to me; flowers too! I loved all of my customers. They encouraged me and even though I'm sure they had no idea, I looked to most of them for advice and guidance. I was forever having issues with Hakeem and as you see a few other guys too. School got harder and being a young mother was dispiriting. Since a lot of them were much older than me, they all had some pretty good stories and advice; I was in need of some damn good advice.

Mike was a regular customer for as long as I had been working there. I could tell he was a charmer; always smiling and blowing kisses my way, I never took any of it personal. I figured he just wanted to make

**Perseverance is Remembrance**

me smile and he did. Mike was a dark chocolate, thick boned, dreaded haired brother with a smile harmful to my soul. He had gold teeth too! He wasn't aware that I thought he was sexy and that I was extremely attracted to him and I wanted to keep it that way. He was into the *heating and cooling* business, and like a lot of the customers we serviced, he was always looking for side work. The way the economy had fallen, it was rough for everyone. It was a coincidence that my mom's furnace completely stopped working; I saw it more as an opportunity.

One day when Mike came in to order some parts, I told him about my mom's furnace problem and he seemed more than happy to help out. We exchanged numbers so that he could get in touch with her. After taking a look at the unit, he was confident that he could fix it with no problem and he did just that. My mom, for some reason, took an immediate liking to Mike and asked what his story was. She was curious as to why we never dated. She noticed he liked me by the way he lit up whenever she mentioned my name. Mike and I only talked a few times, and while he hinted that he liked me, he would always keep his distance. I never questioned him about his personal life. I could tell he had someone special in his life.

It wasn't until about two years later when he disclosed to me that he was in a relationship since the day we met, however they were really going through some hard times for quite sometime. He said that once meeting me he instantaneously wanted to get to know me but he didn't think it would've been fair to drag me into such a mess. That was good enough for because I wasn't up for any more *crazy girlfriends*. By that point, there were no feelings between Mike and me so it was nothing but respect from then on. He continued to come into my job for parts, blow his kisses and call to check on me and my mom. Another two years rolled by and we were still distant associates.

**Perseverance is Remembrance**

Summer was almost over so before school resumed for my daughter, I took her on vacation. Mike called to ask me out for drinks; unfortunately I wasn't in town and therefore had to get a rain check. I was shocked after the fact because it was four years later and he had never asked me out. I assumed he and his girlfriend couldn't stand the storm and were no longer dating. After my vacation ended, it was back home, school time for both me and my daughter and work everyday.

One evening when I was bored, I remembered the rain check from Mike, so I called to see what he was up to. He didn't answer right away however he sent me pictures of beautiful palm trees, high rise resorts and sandy beaches. He was in Puerto Rico. I thought to myself "What a way to celebrate a break up!" We texted one another a few more times during his stay there but by looking at the pictures he sent, I figured he could've been doing better things. I wanted him to enjoy himself and told him I will talk to him whenever he got

**Perseverance is Remembrance**

back home. A few months later Mike called me for the first time since his trip. He wanted to come by and see me. I had just finished cleaning around the house, so I said "Sure."

Meanwhile, I called a friend to come over and sit with me before he arrived. Four years was quite some time, but I did not know him well enough to be inviting him over to my house without having a back up. It didn't take him long to get there and everything went fine; nothing to be alarmed about. After my friend saw that she wasn't going to be seeing me on the ten o'clock news, she decided to leave. Mike and I talked about work along with other things that didn't matter to me. I was more interested in knowing his relationship status because he had thrown me a curve ball by asking me out. He assured me it was nothing for me to be concerned about but I thought just the opposite. This wasn't like Mike so I knew something was up. He said he was going through some paperwork issues with his lady. I automatically

**Perseverance is Remembrance**

assumed he had gotten her pregnant and things didn't work out. I jokingly said "Child support huh?" That was not the case at all.

Mike was in Puerto Rico celebrating his recent wedding. Yes, he was on his honeymoon. He said the paperwork was for his divorce but he really meant things were going sour already. I stood there in disbelief the entire time. This man had been in a *rocky* relationship with this woman for over ten years, decided to marry her, and now was standing in my living room not even three months after their wedding telling me he wanted a divorce. All I could say is "Why?" I never got a real answer from him except for he just wasn't happy. What I didn't understand was why he hadn't told me about any of this especially the marriage. What was the big secret? We had never dated, kissed or even hugged. Mike left my house that night after telling me he had basically waited four years to get close to me. He said he knew his marriage was a mistake and that he wished things were different. He claimed he somehow fell in

**Perseverance is Remembrance**

love with me over the course of our professional relationship and he wanted to see what else was possible, personally. I left the room to take a look in the mirror because I thought I had *deaf, dumb and stupid* written on my forehead. I had to give him a piece of my mind. I wasn't *deaf, dumb or stupid*. I didn't want to share my guy with another woman and that was exactly what he was proposing. I couldn't bare the thought of another woman knocking on my door with evidence that her husband was between my sheets, I had been down this road before and made it out safely. I escorted him to the front door and told him to have a good night. I was too good for that; I thought. It would've been easier to hit the delete button on him in my phone. Unfortunately I didn't do that.

After Mike left that night, I tried to figure out a way to sleep with him and not feel bad about it; no luck. I completely ignored the advice my mom had given me on married men. Turns out deaf, dumb and stupid was written all over my face.

**Perseverance is Remembrance**

The very next evening a girlfriend of mine asked me to go to *happy hour* and the way I was feeling, I needed something to distract me from my evil thoughts. We had a great time, talked and laughed about our issues with men. This was the same friend who came over to sit with me when Mike came over. I told her the situation and asked her what she thought of it. She was all for it! It shocked the hell out of me; I didn't know if it was the drinks talking or what, but she wasn't helping me at all. She dropped me off at home later that night; I took a shower and went straight to bed. Minutes into my sleep, Mike called to ask if he could come over and before I knew it he was at my door.

My conscious flew out the window. Without any words, Mike walked through my front door; I jumped on him and wrapped my legs around him like a stripper on a pole trying to make ends meet. I quickly escorted him to my bedroom and he ripped off the little clothes I did have on. He had already told me him and his wife

**Perseverance is Remembrance**

weren't living together, so by it being late, I wasn't worried about him getting caught. As nervous as I was, my body was completely in control; with the help of the many *Strawberry Long Islands* from the bar earlier. I could tell he had been drinking because the smell of *Remy* was all over him.

    We got right to it, as music played in the background, he touched every inch of my body; starting with the top of my head and everything in between, he ended with the tip of my toes. His touch was very soft but demanding; he knew exactly how he wanted my body and he got it there. He was in complete control until it was time to go in for the kill. Long story short, it was a disaster. Five dried up condoms thrown in the trash in the matter of minutes after we got done, or shall I say after we never got started. I was mad as hell; I already knew I was going to hell for this, but damn. He apologized, repeatedly but I just saw it as a sign. I had no business with this married man. Mike assured me that it was it nerves

**Perseverance is Remembrance**

that conquered over his ability to perform. He said he had never stepped out on his wife; in the two months they were married. He promised to get it right the next time around. I wasn't looking forward to a "next time." But we did do it again and he got it right. Surprisingly, Mike and I spent more time talking and laughing than we did having sex. I didn't want to develop feelings for him; I knew once that happened, it would be a problem. I distanced myself from Mike for weeks; no phones calls or anything. I knew Mike had no intentions on leaving his wife and honestly, I didn't want him to; not for me. I figured if he would do it to her, he would surely do it to me.

Mike showed up on my door step one evening. He knew I was home because I failed to park my car in the garage. I opened the door only to see gifts galore for me and my daughter. It was flattering but cliché. I knew he missed me but this *thing* between us wasn't working. I should have never crossed that line with him. I rejected him that night but that didn't do any good.

**Perseverance is Remembrance**

He was persistent and he wanted to be the man in my life. He took care of everything; things I am sure his wife needed him for. My bills were paid; if needed, broken things around the house got fixed and he even took care of me when I was sick. One Sunday morning, I could barely roll over; I wasn't sure how I had gotten sick so suddenly. Mike called and as soon as I told him I wasn't feeling well, he rushed right over with breakfast in his hands and an empty lap for me to rest my head in.

He was good at what he did but it did nothing but drive me crazy. I was secretly torturing myself by dealing with this man; I couldn't even enjoy him. I know for a fact a man can't make two women happy and if he could, it wouldn't last long. Mike's wife wasn't happy and neither was I. I was battling many demons from the relationships I previously had and at the end of the day, I concluded my self worth was much more. I allowed a man to confine me to the narrow space of four walls; the same four walls that spoke to me when no

**Perseverance is Remembrance**

one was around and I did not want to hear about another mistake I had made. I was responsible for limiting and depriving another woman of the happiness she rightfully deserved.

# 10
## ~Support Me, Support Me Not~

Hakeem and I weren't *friends* like before, but it was a work in progress. Since the settlement, he called more often so that was a start. I tried my best to include him in the raising of our daughter; he still lived out of town. He was up to date on her school activities, karate class, and her health and so forth.

It had been a *long* nine months of continuous payments he had been making for child support. Month number ten rolled around and that was all she wrote. It wasn't until I noticed that he was two months behind when I began to inquire. He told me he just didn't have it anymore. Ms. Loretta was, God help her soul, still around. I don't think she ever like the fact that Hakeem was ordered to pay and I thanked God daily

**Perseverance is Remembrance**

that it wasn't up to her. She never admitted it, but it was always the way she carried on since day one that wasn't too tasteful.

    Hakeem said he was in between teams and he could no longer afford the amount that he was ordered to pay, which was okay with me. I was still working and I didn't see it as much of a loss, I just knew I would have to adjust a few things pertaining to our daughters activities. I assumed that since he wasn't playing, he would be coming home more often to help me out. Guess I assumed wrong. Ms. Loretta said she had no intentions on allowing Hakeem to move back home. At that point, I noticed it was more of a "status" thing with her. I didn't care if he worked or not. Like I said before, it was important to me that our child was able to receive if not both financial and physical support than obviously one or the other was a must from both sides. Unless Hakeem was signing with another team soon, I needed for him to be here helping me out. We hadn't argued in a long time, but I wanted Hakeem to understand what was important. And the fact that we were awarded *joint custody*, and up until now, I had her, a majority of his time was unacceptable. A lot of issues we had stemmed from the simple fact that Hakeem couldn't make sound decisions. I found myself discussing more issues with Ms. Loretta than I liked. Eventually I was forced to pull our daughter from the activities she grew to love and the school where she had made friends. I even had to submit a letter of apology to her doctor's office for outstanding medical bills that Hakeem was responsible for.

The time came for Ms. Loretta and me to put our differences aside. It was no secret that we weren't each others' favorite but in reality there was absolutely no reason for us to hate one another. I got over the fact that she was horrible. During that entire year, Ms. Loretta took up Hakeem's slack. Between she, me and my mom, nothing was impossible and I got a lot of work done. Ms. Loretta had the baby much

**Perseverance is Remembrance**

more often than usual, took her to doctor appointments, helped her with homework and kept her happy when I was away. It was a much needed and nice gesture as the grandmother. I started to feel like she wasn't so bad after all. We hung out, went on trips and talked much more on a more personal level with one another. We confided in each other and gained what I thought was a mutual respect for one another. It became crucial for me to have this kind of relationship with her over Hakeem because her added help relieve the stresses of balancing it all. I enjoyed that our relationship was growing beyond just the worry of the baby.

It had gotten to a point when I noticed that Ms. Loretta was getting sick. She was taking leave from work because her blood pressure was on the rise. She had a lot on her plate; dealing with a stressful marriage, working long hours, being the sole provider for her household, and supporting all three of her children. Hakeem was her oldest; she had a son in college, and a small daughter

**Perseverance is Remembrance**

three years older than my child. So much was going on and she was going above and beyond to keep it all together. She told me that she was in a financial war, and was close to losing her home. She explained that upon entering the NFL, Hakeem paid her house off however the taxes were delinquent. I felt absolutely horrible because when she asked for help, I couldn't offer anything.

Not too long after, she came back in distress about how she was about to lose her luxury car due to late payments. I had no idea that any of this was going on because every time we were together, she was spending money. But after a while it all came together for me. The only reasonable explanation was that now that Hakeem wasn't playing football anymore Ms. Loretta couldn't afford her lifestyle. I didn't have much to give her since my hours had been drastically cut at work but I managed to scrape up a few hundred dollars, even though she was thousands behind. I guess a part of me felt obligated to her since she

**Perseverance is Remembrance**

began to play an active role in my child's life.

My mom didn't like what she saw was happening and advised me to be careful. She didn't want me getting caught up in anything; she'd forgiven Ms. Loretta for all the years of shit she had caused, she just wasn't convinced that she was genuine and figured there was a motive. I, on the other hand, felt like my mom didn't understand the high road she and I had taken to assure a positive rapport. It was soon after the car deal when someone came to Ms. Loretta's house to summons Hakeem to court. It was a few days later when she told me about it; she was angry because she thought it was me who sent them there for the arrearages he owed for child support. She informed me that it had been exactly two years since Hakeem actually played and that she was the one supporting him; paying his bills and keeping him fed. She went on to say that she would not stand by and let anyone take him to jail for not being able to afford to pay child support for a child that was well taken care of anyway. I first, told her that it wasn't me who called anyone to complain about Hakeem's failure to pay. And if I did, I had every right. Secondly, it was the city that was disputing the delinquent taxes owed on the home and yes they summoned Hakeem to court for it.

When Hakeem paid the home off, he turned it over in his name so he was held responsible. She concluded by asking me to terminate the court order against Hakeem. She stood firm on the belief that I was the one in control of this matter and I was the only one who could put it to rest. I was sick to my stomach that it was a single woman of three children fathered by three different men who claimed she didn't receive help from any of them, asking me to be okay with not having the help I was *rightfully* entitled to. I was in no position to feel sorry for Hakeem especially since his dirty laundry was aired all over the internet by women who were upset about his failed promises to them. Many of those women

**Perseverance is Remembrance**

discussed how he spent thousands of dollars on them; money that could've been saved for rainy days. Some were even embarrassed to say how he slept with them one day and was gone the next. Terminating the court order was not an option. Seems as if he had no intentions on helping from the start had I not asked for it. Our lawyers before, raped us in expenses and I refused to be put in that situation again. This set order was in the best interest of our child, not our inabilities to make responsible decisions. I was the last person to have control over anything. If you ask me, Hakeem could have gotten another job if he wanted to; it didn't have to be with the NFL; Walmart was always looking for greeters. And had he considered coming home on a consistent schedule then I may have considered releasing the order but my hands were tied.

    I was blessed to have graduated from college, earning my Arts degree in Psychology. It was a very emotional time for me after remembering what it took for

**Perseverance is Remembrance**

me to get there. I walked across the stage gracefully as if it were a breeze. I knew that with all I had experienced, I was capable of doing anything. The complications with the economy caused a lot of companies to lay off thousands of employees and perform drastic cut backs. Although I wasn't a victim of the *lay offs*, working zero to twenty hours a week wasn't paying the bills. I had creditors calling daily, wanting money that was owed to their companies. I exhausted all of my options within my company and when I saw no open doors, I left my job and never turned back. Now that I had a degree, I applied with other companies but nothing was happening for me.

I was educated with a six year old child, had a home and car with bills to go with it and no money. I had no idea what I was going to do. Applying for state assistance was by far the hardest thing I ever had to do. It was demeaning having a stranger looking at me as if I were a failure while they counted every penny in my pocket. I sucked it up because it was for my daughter

**Perseverance is Remembrance**

and not just for me. My landlord had been working with me during those troubling times but eventually asked me to vacate my home. Soon after that my car was taken. I began to rely solely on my mom, once again. I had no money, no place of my own to call home and no transportation to get my daughter to and from school.

    I waited, but eventually told my mom the latest drama with Ms. Loretta and Hakeem. She wasn't surprised; she didn't know what but she knew they were up to something, whether it was planned or not. I hadn't spoken to Ms. Loretta or Hakeem for months after that conversation took place. He would call every now and then but the energy that we exerted into each other had been nothing but negative and so I would keep my distance. I did however call him when it was time for our daughter to go to the doctor. She had been struggling with her asthma, a respiratory illness she was diagnosed with months before. I was stunned to find out that she couldn't be serviced because of an outstanding medical bill I was sure had been covered by Hakeem's insurance. I explained to him that it needed to be paid and this is what he said, "I was responsible for that when I was making that type of money years ago, now I haven't been and since you won't cancel the case, it's leaving me with nothing."

**Perseverance of Remembrance**

# ~The End for You; the Beginning for Me~

I was in *Forest Park* one sunny afternoon, walking my dog. It was a beautiful spring day.

As I watched Champ chase his shadow in the pond, I looked up and saw what appeared to be a young black family walking my way, across the bridge. This was rare, since most young, black women I saw would usually walk with their children, alone. Their body language didn't say "family"; there was no laughter, closeness, or love. The woman walked many feet ahead of the little girl who held her daddy's hand. I just thought it was nice to see them together. And just for a second, I wished I had that. When the woman spotted me by the water, she wasted no time making her way over to me. She first complimented on how great Champ, my pit bull, looked and then proceeded to admire my short blonde cut; some referred to as an *Amber Rose*. I wanted to pay her a compliment as well but it was not easy. After getting past the *pink extensions* in her head and the foul language, I found her to be even brighter than she thought she was.

I could tell that she was uncomfortable with this guy standing less than five feet away from her and as soon as he and the little girl walked away, she turned her back to them, faced me and began to cry. It was no secret that she was unhappy and this was why. She bared two children for this thirty-one year old man whom she loved. They lived together in their own apartment; both with jobs and food to eat yet she couldn't understand why he cheated on her. She was aware of his unfaithful tendencies and tried that much harder to be everything he wanted but it was never enough. She definitely dumped a lot on me in the first five minutes of us meeting. My first question for her was "What is your name?" Her reply was "Well, I answer to *Bitch.*" I then asked her what she did for a living. She said

**Perseverance is Remembrance**

she and her boyfriend worked for the same company and she hated her job because she worked with the same women that slept in her bed; she was familiar with the scents. My last question for her was "How much do you make?" She said "Not enough."

She was only twenty-two years old and I was in disbelief that she was younger than me. She looked as if she were living through some real rough times. Her hair was completely damaged with *weave and glue*, her breasts sagged and she had many endless layers of dead skin on the heels of her feet. She explained to me that she was a victim of group homes as a child and when she was lucky enough to be placed in foster care, she really wasn't so lucky at all. She never knew either of her parents and because of the experiences in her life she didn't want her children to go through the same thing. She said she was doing everything in her power to assure that both of her kids' parent's were together. And while that was a touching story, look at the price she had to pay for it.

**Perseverance is Remembrance**

Every tear that fell from that girl's face represented every *bitch*, hoe and slut she was called by her unfaithful man. She felt less special by the slightest touch of him because he touched every other woman the same way. I wondered what exactly she was losing by not having him around. It was evident that she had done badly before him and she certainly didn't need his help to do bad now. She said she was on a search to reunite with God. She **demanded** that he find favor over her relationship with this guy and see them through.

One thing I will say is that throughout all of the experiences in my life, even now as I move forward, I've learned that when I go to God, I go to him with nothing; as nothing. I don't know what to ask for anymore and therefore I ask for his *will*. My prayer is simple, "Lord, give me what you see fit for me to have." That was my advice to that woman. How can anyone **demand** anything when they can't deliver something equal of themselves? Like Steve Harvey, I believe the three essential areas for any

**Perseverance is Remembrance**

persons to focus on, are "who you are, what you do, and how much you make." Judging by the answers that young lady gave me in the park, she needed some new goals. Confidence shines through self adequacy and if you have no confidence your self worth appears less valued.

If you have ever experienced any lie, any heart break or hardship in general, then you understand the essence of a *struggle*. We sometimes hurt even more when people don't understand exactly why we are hurting. For many years I blamed Ms. Loretta for the malfunction of Hakeem's loyalty to me, and I didn't understand why he couldn't see that his child and I were affected by her need to be in charge. I was even more upset because of his inconsideration; as if he simply didn't care that I was angry or how stressed I'd become over raising this child alone. I learned that no matter what we do in life, we will be held accountable for every action, every lie, every truth, and every good and bad. We have more control over the fate of own lives

**Perseverance is Remembrance**

than we own. Carlos, Nate, Tony and Mike were all seasons; it was cold, rainy, sunny and windy. They came, they went, and I learned. As for Hakeem, it's going to be a long winter.

Although I have never been raped, a member of any gang or juggled throughout foster care, I still have a story. I'm no *basketball wife* and I don't drive luxury cars. It does get discouraging at times as a single parent. And anyone out there who says this job is easy, they are even more stressed no matter how much they earn, with trying to keep up this image. But with all of the tears shed, the sleepless nights, and the never ending bills that come along with life, there are the smiles that light up my world every time my daughter says "Mama, I love you." It's not her that shouldn't get to experience a wonderful childhood because Hakeem and I can't find common ground to compromise with one another. The great thing about life is that once you make a mistake, you don't stop living. I have a piece of mind knowing that I'm not creeping around here with

**Perseverance is Remembrance**

another woman's husband. I sleep well at night because I'm not getting tested every other week for the AID's virus because I loved one man while he loved another man. It's good to know that when someone asks me my name, *"Bitch"* is not even the last thing on my list. I have a mother who loved me enough to stay, I had a father who loved me enough to leave, I have a friend who hears my every cry and I have a daughter who believes me to be the best mommy in the world. I strive to *remember me.*

*"If anybody ever wondered when they would see the sun up, just remember when you come up, the show goes on."-Lupe Fiasco*

**Perseverance of Remembrance**

*Almost free from the chain…*

**Perseverance is Remembrance**

# *Letter to You*

*Dear Reader,*

*You may wonder how I stayed with Nate, a gay man. You may hate me for willingly sleeping with a married man. You may even be thinking how stupid it was of me to give Ms. Loretta anything after the way she treated me. If I were you, I would think those very same things. Late at night as I lay in bed, many thoughts rush through my head. I think about the weak and strong; I question all the right and wrong. Life doesn't come with all of the answers but it does overwhelm us with questions.*

*Although my mom was good to me; she pushed me in a forward direction and always advised me to do right, somehow I went left. I was a beautiful young girl with everything going for me however I made a few choices that have severely affected my life today. I wonder who I could really be; I think of what's gotten into me. I hung out with the entirely wrong crowd and all of these thoughts I am thinking out loud.*

*I've been told that I give Hakeem too much "slack". Some question if I am still in love with him. I hear stories everyday of how women hate the father's of their children and tear down their character, bitter because of the fact they are either not together, he's moved on, or because he is not taking on the role of the responsible father. Honestly, I was bitter; I was upset because I didn't understand*

**Perseverance is Remembrance**

why my relationship with Hakeem had failed. Was it because of our unplanned pregnancy? Or was it because of his deceitful mother? To tell you the truth, no, Hakeem still does not pay child support nor does he see his child.

What is this life I am in? My head was beginning to spin. I paced my room without a sound, walking in circles around and around. All these questions, I ask myself, I can never finish a single task, my heart beats really fast whenever I ask myself "will this really last?" I realized that walking around with a bitter attitude does not pay any of my bills, nor does it help feed my daughter.

"Once you accept who you are, you are no longer lying and hiding who you are." These were words spoken by J.L. King, one of the first men to step forward about his "down low" lifestyle. People say there is no way a woman could know that her man is gay. This could be true, but in my case, I knew. Clearly, I had so many signs. It was my own self who refused to see what was right in front of my eyes. Nate wasn't a bad guy; he also wasn't true to himself and therefore couldn't be true to me. I loved the way he treated me; held my hand in public, opened car doors and wasn't afraid to stand up for me. I was in love with the ideal of how Nate treated me rather than who he really was. Nothing I did felt right, even though I am very bright. Why did it feel this way? It was the exact same thing everyday.

There is just no excuse for Mike. Sleeping with a married man not only takes something away from others but it also

**Perseverance is Remembrance**

*diminishes important things from your own character and lowers your self esteem. I am ashamed and I am sorry. So here I am, thinking in my head, all the negative things I've done. This is not the real me, it definitely cannot be.*

*It's not sad to say that if I had to do it all over again to get where I am today, I would. My experiences have given me the opportunity to learn the true meaning of right and wrong. I have just helped someone by being someone I truly am not. It's not okay to let a man hit you, it's not okay to sleep around, and it's not okay for you not to understand your self worth.*

*If you found yourself pissed at me, good. If you felt sorry for me, I don't need sympathy. Empathize with me. Know that I had choices and you do too. I have made myself vulnerable to you, not to be judged but to be an inspiration. Sitting here thinking for a while, now I find myself beginning to smile. All of these emotions I have to express, finally letting go of all this stress.*

*I think of all the positive things, hurt feels like a man constantly beating on me. Life isn't something I can find in a tree, it's only what's inside of me. Always remember that perseverance is the continued effort to do or achieve something despite difficulty, failure or opposition. My continued effort to persevere through my hardships; heartbreaks, lies and deceit, could serve as inspiration for you to be better than I was, as strong as I am and together we will be more powerful than ever.*

**Perseverance is Remembrance**

# *Free from the chain…*

*Sincerely Yours,*

*Aigner Y. Martin*

Made in the USA
Charleston, SC
28 November 2011